**A STUDY GUIDE
COMMENTARY**

THE PASTORAL EPISTLES

BOOKS IN THE "STUDY GUIDE" SERIES . . .

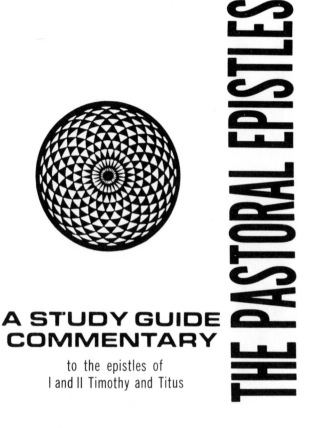

**A STUDY GUIDE
COMMENTARY**

to the epistles of
I and II Timothy and Titus

THE PASTORAL EPISTLES

E. M. BLAIKLOCK

**ZONDERVAN
PUBLISHING HOUSE** OF THE ZONDERVAN CORPORATION
GRAND RAPIDS, MICHIGAN 49506

THE PASTORAL EPISTLES
© 1972 by The Zondervan Corporation
Grand Rapids, Michigan

Library of Congress Catalog Card Number: 74-180838

Sixth printing 1979
ISBN 0-310-21233-2

Printed in the United States of America

CONTENTS

THE PASTORAL EPISTLES

A STUDY GUIDE
COMMENTARY

INTRODUCTION

A. *The Project*

"There is no substitute," said a president of Harvard a few years ago, "for staying with one small area of knowledge until it is mastered." This is true of the study of the Bible, as in every other field. There is too commonly a resort to the superficial. "Outline studies," "synoptic studies," "rapid surveys" of books and themes, "digests" and "summaries," no doubt, have their place, but if such study has its use it is only when joined with detailed attention to one portion or theme. And this applies to the study of the Bible, as it does to every other field of serious reading and study.

If their faith is to stand firm and informed among the thronging heresies of our day, Christians must know the Word. They must be familiar with doctrine and tradition. They must know what their faith is and what it is not. It matters what they believe, as the words of Paul in these three most relevant and significant epistles make most abundantly clear.

A vast literature has gathered around the Bible, and while it is quite true that what the Bible itself says is of far greater importance than anything which can be said about it, the background of what we read and study has supreme importance. These studies will make every endeavor to be complete in themselves, but will also bear in mind the many who are prepared to read more widely, and to buy some basic books. All serious Bible students should accumulate a reference library, and one of the aims of the study-notes which follow will be to indicate where material relevant to the epistles before us will be found. It is important to know, and to use such aids.

For example, Donald Guthrie has a fine little commentary in the Tyndale New Testament Series, which might most usefully be acquired as a basic book. It is "informed conservatism" at its best. William Barclay's commentary from the Westminster Press is useful and informative. It is to be confessed that, in some of his New Testament commentaries, this scholar strays, on rare occasions, into lines of interpretation not acceptable to conservative scholarship, but he is useful for the mass of his comment, is beyond reproach in the notes on the pastoral epistles, and is impeccable in his classical, linguistic and historical scholarship.

Reference will also be made to the *Expositor's Greek Testament,* edited by W. Robertson Nicoll (Eerdmans), for those who have at least a smattering of New Testament Greek. Even an hour's work learning the Greek alphabet will allow one to pronounce a word in Greek script, and will usefully open up important reference works, which can be found in church or public libraries. The study of the Bible is the duty of all who follow Christ, but no one need imagine that a true knowledge of Scripture is acquired without effort, a zeal to learn, to know and understand, along with the discipline of mind and reading which all study demands. Intellectual as well as spiritual stimulus is the reward. To grow in Christ, a Christian must know the Word of God. Lack of desire to grow in Christ is sickness of the soul.

B. *The Principles*

To understand any document, certain principles should guide initial study: (1) *Who* wrote the text? (2) *When* was it written and under what circumstances? (3) To *whom* was it written? (4) *What* was the purpose of writing, what needs or preoccupations on the part of the recipient occasioned the communication? If these matters are established, the primary purpose of the document is in view.

In Scripture there is always a secondary meaning. The Word is an utterance of the Eternal God, as well as a communication of man. Paul was writing to Timothy. In the same act, God was speaking to the Church. This must be the theme of our deeper study, but it must nevertheless follow the discovery, as far as is possible, of the author's original purpose.

THE TEXT

A. *The Writer*

There is no reason to doubt the Pauline authorship of these epistles. Arguments against their authenticity, based on the precarious criteria of vocabulary and style, are surveyed in the article on the Pastoral Epistles in the *Zondervan Pictorial Bible Dictionary*.

Recent attempts to upset the traditional view of the Pauline authorship, based on computer techniques, need not be taken seriously. Observe: (i) A computer is an instruction-taking machine, and produces only the digested results of the data fed into it. The programming remains at the subjective stage. (ii) The possible data could only be statistics of word-usage, the incidence of certain parts of speech, the structures of syntax, and quirks of grammar, in so far as these are reducible to figures, and such measurable material. Anyone who writes much is conscious of changes in style according to the subject, the recipient, self-awareness and its effect upon the use of words, mannerisms, haste, and the hundred devices by which a writer modifies consciously his own form of writing. (iii) The amanuensis, who took the letter from dictation, may have played a part. In his introduction to his highly original translation of the New Testament epistles, A. S. Way develops a theory of "note style," which, he plausibly argues, accounts for some of Paul's disconcerting brevities and ellipses. Without going so far as fully to accept this theory, it is quite possible that one who knew Paul's mind could be left to phrase in his own words a passage of the letter. The authority of the text would in no way be impugned. Paul would hear it read back and sanction it. These and other factors make nonsense of certain computerized conclusions.

Other arguments against Paul's authorship allege that the development of a church organization was too advanced for the seventh decade. This is untenable. Paul was working hard to establish a firm structure. To believe in order was part of his Romanitas, that aspect of his citizenship which saw the Empire as a framework for his evangelism, and its peace and law as God's gift to the world (See 1 Tim. 5:1, 17-19; 3:1-7, 8-13; Titus 1:5-16.)

The fact that the beginnings of Gnosticism were finding shape in a speculative intellectualism, if that contention be correctly deduced from the epistles to Timothy, is no argument against Pauline authorship. Paul could have given more than one example of the speed with which a deviant view of Christianity can form and cohere. He might have quoted the letters to Corinth, Galatia, and Colossae. (See 1 Tim. 1:4; 6:4; 2 Tim. 2:4, 23; Titus 2:11; 3:9.)

There is a considerable preliminary task in reading about Paul himself. A rapid review of the biographical detail is nonetheless necessary. Read the articles on the apostle in the *Zondervan Pictorial Bible Dictionary* (henceforth referred to as *P.B.D.*).

B. *The Date of the First Epistle to Timothy*

Material for wider and more detailed study will be found under "Pastoral Epistles" in *P.B.D.* (6 *Chronology*, p. 625). Donald Guthrie's terse and comprehensive introduction in *Commentary on the Pastoral Epistles (Tyndale New Testament Commentaries)* also surveys the material well.

The epistle was written (and this theory is supported by ancient tradition) after the first Roman imprisonment. Contrary to the views of some liberal commentators, tradition cannot be lightly dismissed. Nor does internal evidence contradict the traditional belief. The date, while it must

NOTE: (1) the point in Paul's career when he met Timothy (read the relevant passages in Acts 16); (2) where he met him (read the article on Lystra in a Bible dictionary).

lack complete precision, is somewhere after Paul's presumed release in late A.D. 62 or 63, and before the political persecution which followed Nero's measures against the Christians of Rome in late A.D. 64, which began with the Great Fire of Rome, in July, 64. It may be supposed that Paul's second arrest (at Troas?) and his subsequent death, took place in A.D. 67. Set A.D. 65 as a reasonable date for the epistle.

C. *The Recipient of the Epistles to Timothy*

(Read about Timothy in *P.B.D.* or some similar reference work.) Paul saw in the able young man a ready pupil for his global gospel. Timothy was free from the prejudices and outlook of metropolitan Judaism, of mixed parentage, and therefore sympathetic toward the Hellenized Judaism which was peculiarly Paul's own. Conscious of no "generation gap," he made the young man his close companion, and promoted him, with some misgivings on Timothy's part, to positions of importance. At the time of the writing of this letter, Timothy held a position of trust in Ephesus (1:1-3), where Paul hoped to rejoin him. Save for a subsequent experience of imprisonment (Heb. 13:23), Timothy's later history is unknown.

It will be a useful exercise to order and interpret the references in Acts (chapters 16, 20), and the letters to the Corinthians (1 Cor. 1:4-17; 16:10, 11; 2 Cor. 2:1-19. Also Rom. 16:21, and 1 Tim. 1:2; 2 Tim. 1:5) which touch on biographical detail. From the letters to Timothy it is possible to form some notion of an affectionate, nervous, loyal person (see also 1 Cor. 16:10; Phil. 2:19 ff). Above all, loyalty was what Paul sought at the time when he chose Timothy to succeed John Mark who had abandoned the great project of evangelism which Paul was prosecuting at the time when the apostle hastened from Perga to the Roman city of Pisidian Antioch (Acts 16:36, 37). (Some wider basic reading could also be done in Donald Guthrie's 50-page introduction, in W. M. Ramsay's *St. Paul the Traveller and the Roman Citizen* (Baker paperback) or

Century of the New Testament (E. M. Blaiklock, Inter-varsity Press).

D. *The First Letter to Timothy*

Simultaneously with the above lines of study, which should be systematically pursued, the epistle should be read twice at a sitting, to gain a clear synoptic view. There is no substitute for a basic familiarity with the text itself. There are at least twenty-seven English versions of the New Testament. First Timothy should be read in RSV, NEB, Moffatt, Weymouth, Goodspeed, Phillips, Living Letters, Jerusalem Bible or almost any other version available.

Those who have some foreign language might read it in French, German, Italian, the Latin Vulgate, or the original Greek. All will provide facets of meaning, for every translation distills ninety-five percent of the original — but all of them offer a different ninety-five percent.

Bible study is a serious business. The associated literature is immense, and good, conservative scholarship has served the epistle well. There is mental stimulus, and absorbing interest, as we have remarked, as well as spiritual inspiration and challenge to be had from this exercise. It is a call to effort, dedication, and disciplined work. Without these basic qualities no scheme of study is possible. Their exercise increases the strength and stature of mind and heart.

I Timothy

I

CHAPTER ONE (1-11)

Introduction and Summary

One of Timothy's tasks at Ephesus was to counter the pernicious activities of those who sought to make the Gospel difficult, took away from ordinary folk the simplicities of God's salvation, and then lost themselves and those they taught in a shadow-world of mystic Old Testament interpretations. Then, as now, those who obscured clear truth, and turned a message God intended to be understood by ordinary men and women into abstruse doctrine, clear only to a select few, were a plague and a peril in the community of Christ. The Bible, in the prayer-book phrase, is meant to be "understanded of the people."

Love, not unedifying speculation and controversy, says verse 5, is the Gospel's first fruit — love springing from a pure heart, a good conscience, and faith unfeigned. Such qualities were not obvious in those who sought to exalt themselves as teachers of "the Law," empty chatterers, bewitched by foolish words (6, 7). "What do they mean by the Law?" Paul asks. The Law is not a clutter of mystic nonsense, but the body of God's commandments, God's condemnation of sin in all its forms. The Law, as Judaism conceived it, had primarily to deal with sin, and was part of a larger concept which found fulfillment in the Gospel of Jesus Christ.

A. *The Salutation: 1:1-2*

1. This is a letter. Its form and shape correspond to the fashion of letter writing in Paul's day. For example, glance

17

at some of the papyrus letters in J. D. Thompson's *The Bible and Archaeology*, or E. M. Blaiklock's *Archaeology of the New Testament* (Zondervan).

2. The normal salutation would, however, have been: "Paul to Timothy, greeting." The elaboration in verse 1 indicates that the letter was formal, and a communication designed to be read in the churches committed to Timothy's care. These are the instructions and guidelines entrusted to one in authority.

Proceed thus:

(a) Go through the chapter identifying statements of theological and doctrinal import.

(b) Note the assumption of apostolic authority. Observe this at the opening of nine of the epistles, and pick the reason for the omission in four (1 and 2 Thessalonians, Philippians and Philemon). Note the variant formula "by the will of God" in the five epistles. Compare also Romans 16:26; 1 Corinthians 7:6; Titus 1:3. Consider this, together with (a) in relation to the emerging pattern of leadership.

(c) Some details of language: *God our Savior*. Westcott, in his famous commentary on John, remarks of this title that it "is confined (with the exception of the writings of St. Luke) to the later writings of the New Testament, and is not found in the central group of Paul's epistles." In Luke the phrase means "God the deliverer," in the Old Testament, rather than the New Testament sense. In Timothy and Titus the emphasis becomes specifically evangelical.

Lord Jesus Christ. Observe the interplay of "Jesus Christ" and "Christ Jesus" in this chapter. Assuming that the former order marks the prominence of the historical figure, and the latter the theological concept in the writer's mind, try to catch the nuance of meaning in the context (vv. 1, 2, 12, 14, 16) which determined each use.

Grace, mercy, peace. Found only here and in 2 Timothy 1:2 and 2 John 3. Grace and peace are the Greek and Hebrew salutations. Mercy is the added Christian touch (Gal. 6:16). Examine the meaning of all three words in an English dictionary, in a Bible dictionary, and in a concordance. Why did Paul wish "mercy" to Timothy and not to Titus? Perhaps he had some small anxieties over Timothy's administrative capacity. Perhaps in Corinth he had not been notably successful. The young and the sensitive stand in such need.

B. *The Charge: 1:3-7*

1. Paul confirms in writing verbal instructions already given. Note the passionate care for the preservation of sound doctrine, the impatience with speculative innovation and tampering, and the confidence of an older man that a well-taught younger man could do what was required.

2. "Teach no other doctrine" is one word in Greek and it occurs again in 6:3. See Galatians 1:6 and 2 Corinthians 11:4. His early foreboding is finding fulfillment in Ephesus (Acts 20:29-30). Paul does not name the innovators. Their doctrine apparently was not a coherent system, but a clutter of "tiresome" (KJV has "endless") lists and names: "Paying attention to myths and interminable genealogies" (Montgomery), "devoting themselves to myths and never-ending pedigrees" (Williams), "busy themselves with stories and endless records of ancestors" (Beck). (These variations are listed in Zondervan's *New Testament in 26 Translations,* another handy reference book for this study.)

(a) Note that the writers of the New Testament knew well enough what myths were. According to scholars in the Bultmannian school they were busy creating myths! Yet they call them "vain jangling"; "empty talk"; "fruitless talking"; "a wilderness of words."

Involved in such heresies were the complications of the Gnostic (see the Bible dictionary for explanation of Gnosticism) imaginings about orders of beings. "Questionings" or speculations without hope of answer, which along with fanciful embroiderings of Hebrew history (the "myths"), formed the stock-in-trade of discussion to the exclusion of "godly edifying" (v. 4), or that divine plan which is revealed in the faith, whose keynotes are in v. 5.

It is the common preoccupation of heresy, from ancient

times to now, to turn theology into a philosophy. To be sure, a philosophy of life can emerge from a soundly based theology, but a philosophy cannot create a theology. The process is likely to end with "the death of God," and the abolition of absolutes, a result all too familiar.

(b) Consider the modern application: Are love, integrity, a good conscience, and true faith still a worthy theme? What of new "myths"? (For further reading see the chapter on "Myth or History" in *Layman's Answer: An Examination of New Theology* by E. M. Blaiklock [Hodder] and *Ring of Truth* by J. B. Phillips [Macmillan]).

(c) Observe that heresy is to be refuted, not by ordered arguments but by positive preaching (vv. 5-7). Paul himself demonstrates that this is not the only way. But it was the way for Timothy in the Ephesian context.

"Heart, conscience, faith" mark a progression. It is sound psychology. The three can be followed up after the fashion of "grace, mercy, peace" in 2(c) above. Note the adjectives: *Pure.* See Matthew 5:8 and 2 Timothy 2:22. The springs of moral insight must not be corrupted.

Good. An emphasis of this is a feature of the Pastorals: (see 1 Tim. 1:19, 3:9; 2 Tim. 1:3. Contrast 1 Tim. 2:4 and 1 Peter 3:16 and Heb. 13:8).

Unfeigned. This literally means "without hypocrisy" (2 Tim. 1:5; Rom. 12:9; 2 Cor. 6:6).

C. *A Further Explanation: 1:9-11*

1. The law is good in a proper context. "Good" is the Greek word which also means "beautiful," for Greek thought always linked beauty with goodness. Paul means that "the Law" is part of universal law, the maker of order, the setter of standards. It is absorbed in the Gospel (see the Sermon on the Mount) for both Law and the Gospel promote uprightness.

2. Observe the stern listing of sins. Has Paul the Decalogue in mind in vv. 9 and 10? Observe, too, the emphasis on sexual perversion. "Sound doctrine" is literally "healthy teaching." Look into the metaphor of mental and

moral health and sickness. See Plato's *Republic* 4:425, 426 and the Collect for St. Luke's Day in the Book of Common Prayer. Plato writes in that famous dialogue:

> You mean that such persons will live as those who are in bad health, and yet, from their want of self-restraint, cannot make up their minds to relinquish a pernicious course of life?
>
> Precisely so.
>
> And truly such people lead a charming life! Always in the doctor's hands, they make no progress, but only complicate and aggravate their maladies; and yet they are always hoping that someone will recommend them a medicine which shall cure them.
>
> Yes, that is just the case with invalids of this kind.
>
> Again, is it not charming that they should regard as their greatest enemy any one who tells them the truth, and assures them that till they give up their drunkenness, gluttony, and debauchery, and laziness, no drugs, nor any use of caustic or the knife, nor yet charms, or amulets, or any thing of the kind, will do them any good?

The Collect runs: "Almighty God, who calledst Luke the Physician . . . to be an evangelist and physician of the soul, may it please Thee that, by the wholesome medicines of the doctrine delivered by him all the diseases of our souls may be healed."

The Stoics believed that sins were diseases and the Areopagus address reveals Paul's sympathy with Stoic thought, and his knowledge of Plato — a fact apparent in the first four chapters of First Corinthians. He uses the same metaphor of health and sickness five times in the pastoral epistles (1 Tim. 6:3; 2:1, 13; Tit. 1:13; 2:2, 8). The early church fathers often described salvation as "healing."

QUESTIONS FOR DISCUSSION

  (i) What are the advantages of:
    (a) synoptic study?
    (b) study in depth?
 (ii) How does the New Testament deal with heresy?
(iii) Why is Bible study "a serious business"?

(iv) What importance has the Old Testament in the study of the New Testament?

(v) Why is it impossible to separate doctrine and ethics?

(vi) Illustrate from other letters Paul's interest in conduct.

(vii) What is humility?

(viii) What have beauty and goodness in common?

(ix) What is "prophecy" in the New Testament?

II

CHAPTER ONE (12-20)

Introduction and Summary

The mention of the Gospel leads Paul into a passage of biography. No one, he felt, could be beyond hope if he who had once fought the faith with word and deed could find mercy. "Chief of sinners," he describes himself, and the tense remains present, as though the apostle could not cast off an abiding sense of personal unworthiness. Similar confession is found in 1 Corinthians 15:9 and Ephesians 3:8, where Paul calls himself "the least of the apostles" and "less than the least of all saints." Most noble spirits are thus aware of their own shortcomings. In proportion as a man lifts his ideals high, in proportion to his conception of Christ's perfection, so will a good man's progress in the life of the Spirit appear to him unworthy of the grace he has received. No one could accuse Paul of being morbid; he never grovelled in remorse. He knew his sin was forgiven, but he never forgot the condition from which he had found deliverance. How different was Christ, and how utterly unlike, in this regard, any saint of earth! Christ never repented, never in word or deed showed any consciousness of personal sin or unworthiness, and nothing more clearly demonstrated that He was different from man, a Being of another sphere. We stand with Paul. We have no righteousness but Christ's.

A. *Doxology: 1:12-17*

Paul opened this letter with a formal salutation, indicating that it was a letter to be read by Timothy to his churches. In it Paul charges Timothy and the churches to preserve sound doctrine and forget idle speculation.

1. Now in vv. 12-17 Paul, as he was apt to do, breaks into the poetry of praise to God. Compare this section with 1 Corinthians 15:9 and Ephesians 3:8 for his personal motive. A similar instance of lofty utterance is 1 Corinthians 13.

2. Some points of language should be noted: *Enabled* (v. 12). "Made me equal to the task" (NEB), "The source of all my strength" (Knox). The same verb is employed in 2 Timothy 2:1, 4:17, Philippians 4:13; Hebrews 11:34. Paul is the only New Testament writer who uses it, apart from Luke in Acts 9:22, where he reflects a statement of Paul — a mark of authentic reporting.

Faithful (v. 12). The word is used eleven times in this epistle. Its basic meaning is "trustworthy." See v. 15 below.

Ministry (v. 12). The Greek is *diakonia,* whence the word "deacon." It means any form of service. First Corinthians 3:5; Second Corinthians 3:6; 5:8; 6:3; Colossians 1:23; Ephesians 3:7 contain the word or its variants. Discuss the "ministry." (There is a carefully written article on the word in the *New Bible Dictionary* [IVF].) Can the specialization of the word be detected in the New Testament (e.g., Rom. 16:1; Phil. 1:1, 1 Tim. 3:8, 12)?

3. In the biographical passage, look up the variants of Paul's description of himself (see various versions, or *The New Testament in 26 Translations*). Note the merging into the evangelical proclamation of vv. 15, 16 and 17.

Faith and love are consistently linked. As J. H. Bernard says, "The best gifts of the grace which is from Christ are faith in Him, and love which, centered in Him, necessarily embraces all the members of that human family whose brotherhood is revealed by the fact of the Incarnation."

Compare Second Timothy 1:13; Ephesians 6:23, First Thessalonians 5:8. Ignatius, Augustine and Bunyan all spoke in similar terms. Such humility is the common language of human piety. Contrast this with the unrepentant holiness of Christ. It is not easy to imagine anyone but Paul penning the description of himself given here. The confession is a badge of authenticity.

4. Look at all three doxologies of the Pastoral Epistles (1 Tim. 1:17, 6:16; 2 Tim. 4:18). A doxology is a formula of reverence and worship. The formula may have been to some extent an established one in the Church (Cf. Heb. 13:21; 1 Peter 4:11, 5:11; Rev. 7:12).

B. *The Charge Repeated: 1:18-20*

1. *The grammar.* Notice in the KJV, at the end of v. 4, the blunt "so do." This supplies an apodosis, that is, a principal clause, for vv. 3-4 are a subordinate clause without a main clause. In a fashion not uncommon with him, Paul has switched from his theme. In verse 18 he reconnects and supplies the main clause. His tumultuous speed of thought is in harness again.

2. *The language.* "The inspired words which pointed to you" is the best translation of verse 18. Silas was with Paul at Lystra (Acts 16:3). Barnabas had been with him previously in the border colony. Both companions could have spoken of Timothy with words which Paul took to be an indication of the divine will.

Follow up "prophecy" in the Bible dictionary. The imagery of soldiering might also be considered, together with "shipwreck" of v. 19. Paul knew something of shipwreck! (Acts 27; 2 Cor. 11:25).

It was a "good campaign" (18) which Timothy was called to engage upon. The word is *kalos* which means "beautiful," as well as good — a typical Greek merging of ideas. It is characteristic of the pastoral epistles (1 Tim. 4:6; 6:12, 13; 2 Tim. 1:14).

3. *The heretics.* For Alexander, see Acts 19:33 and Second Timothy 4:14. There is no guarantee that these were the same men. For Hymenaeus, see Second Timothy 2:17.

The process of excommunication is obscure, but apparently designed to be spiritually corrective (see 1 Cor. 5:5). Whatever was involved, an exclusion from Christian participation and fellowship was certainly a part. Probably Acts 5:1-11, 13:11 are not the situation in view. No correction or rehabilitation is there envisaged.

The KJV here is wrongly ironic. Compare: "that they may be disciplined not to speak profanely" (Berkeley), ". . . stop their abusive speech" (Williams), ". . . not to slander holy things" (Beck). Moffatt's "teach them to stop their blasphemous ongoings!" unnecessarily sharpens the unjustifiable irony of the KJV.

The process was either (a) excommunication after the synagogue precedent, (b) expulsion into "the world," or (c) prayer for physical chastisement.

Barclay is at his leisurely best in his 42-page discussion of this chapter. Donald Guthrie also has 14 useful pages. Both illustrate the helpfulness of a little knowledge of Greek, at least enough to enable the student to use a lexicon.

III

CHAPTER TWO (1-15)

Introduction and Summary

These words were written after Nero's first insane persecution of the Church. Every year saw the young emperor slip more deeply into crime, and the Christians of Rome were not the only ones who lived in fear. The aristocracy and Senate of Rome was to be decimated. The grim events of A.D. 69 were discernible afar. In that dark year four rivals contended for the throne, and Rome tottered on the edge of anarchy. That was the year in which "the Beast was wounded to death," and to the world's wonder, recovered (Rev. 13:3). This is the background of Paul's direction to all men to pray for those in power, "so that our common life may be lived in peace and quiet with a proper sense of God and our responsibility to Him" (2, Phillips). The ideal of a quiet, peaceful, godly and honorable life, is one which might be more steadily remembered in a similar world of toil and turmoil. It is not God's will that His children should live lives of tension, overwork, and strife (3). Indeed, He would have all men know the rest He offers in His one message to the distracted world — that message which found full and final expression in His Son, our Savior. With the thought of quietness and unassuming peace in mind, Paul speaks finally to women, and in the background to his words was the noise, the indecent self-display, the unwomanly carnality, and pernicious influence of the women of Ephesus with its worship of Artemis, and an "emancipated" generation.

The charge to the young leader (1 Tim. 1:18) continues, then, and will open up two lines of study: I. The
place of prayer in the Church; II. The place of women in
the Church.

Read the whole chapter in one or two versions, noting
Paul's manner. The two themes merge into statements of
basic doctrine. Consider this section first as an illustration
of Paul's digressive style of writing. (Locate two other examples, say in the letters to Corinth and Ephesus.)

Then consider it as an indication of Paul's urgent desire
that a church not yet in full possession of the New Testament documents, should have clearly based doctrine for
its guidance.

Thirdly, consider the chapter as a pointer toward a
fundamental fact of Christianity: conduct and belief are
linked. Recently two Berkeley sociologists investigated the
relation of belief to the practice of religion. They concluded
"that a demythologized modernism is overwhelming the
traditional Christ-centered faith," in some segments of the
Church, and that traditional belief lies beneath all other
forms of commitment, attendance at church, the practice of
prayer and Christian charity. Christians have never believed
anything else, but it is sometimes of interest to see a secular
survey reach the obvious conclusions.

1. *Verse 1*

Four words cover the nature of prayer:

(a) *Supplications.* The word means an earnest request,
and implies a sense of indigence, helplessness and need. The
Lord's Prayer contains a request for the day's food, a request which may have lost some of its edge in affluent
modern households, but one which is still sharply felt in
poverty-stricken lands.

(b) *Prayers.* This is better translated "humble en-
treaties." While the first word (a) could perhaps be used of
a request from man to man, the second word (b), one of
the most universal words in the New Testament for prayer,
can only be used of a request made to God.

The two words, (a) and (b), in reverse order, occur again in First Timothy 5:5; Ephesians 6:18; Philippians 4:6. Pause to list desires which you might express under the first head and those more properly expressed by the second.

(c) *Intercessions.* The word originally meant an encounter, a meeting with another. The notion of conversation grew out of this, and then an interview with someone in authority.

Read the story of Esther's coming into the presence of Artaxerxes, and First John 2:28 in Phillips' striking translation. It is the Christian's privilege to enter, in his Lord's name, into the presence of the Most High.

(d) *Giving thanks.* The word means precisely this. Joyous thanksgiving is praise and it should accompany all prayer (Phil. 4:6; Col. 4:2).

Paul's purpose in this multiplication of terms should be considered. Remember that any interpretation which makes Scripture remote or difficult, and makes devotion complicated, is likely to be mistaken. Paul wrote to be understood. He had no desire to make prayer self-conscious or unnatural. This is rhetoric, not doctrine. Although the various forms of prayer comprehended under these words cover the various forms of private and public prayer, and although the terms themselves are not interchangeable, Paul was making no formal classification of the deepest exercise of the human spirit. It is obvious that "thanksgivings" cannot be offered for all men. Paul's purpose was emphasis. *All* kinds of prayer were and are relevant in *all* situations. "All" is repeated in 1:2. Paul was fond of the word. It was a spark from the fire of his conviction that the Gospel was for all men. See Philippians 1:7-9. Note, too, that the varied aspects of prayer covered in his multiple enumeration, all find illustration in the Lord's prayer.

2. *Verse 2*

We have anticipated the theme a little. Remember that the "king" was Nero, or some puppet such as those of the Herod family, set up by Rome. Paul's concept of the Empire underlay his evangelistic program. Luke's "second treatise" had as one of its purposes the vindication of Christianity as no hostile or seditious force, but a cement for society. It was a notion derived from Paul.

Look at the strategic points on a map at which Paul set up his Christian cells (see *Century of the New Testament* and *Commentary on Acts* [IVF] by E. M. Blaiklock).

It is the business of authority to provide peace and security. It is the business of the Church to cement the social structure by upright living — "in full observance of religion and high standards of morality" (NEB).

The second word ("honesty" — KJV) contains the notions of dignity, seriousness and earnestness. It is the Latin *gravitas,* and in the seventeenth century "honesty" meant something like this. It was "seemliness" or "decorum" in behavior. A Christian's bearing and conduct are contained in the word. A man who is *semnos* (and this is the Greek adjective) manifests a proper reserve on all occasions but a reserve which contains the elements of strength and decision. He enjoys good fellowship without playing the fool. He shuns extremes, extravagance, insincerity in manners and conversation. (Look up John Henry Newman's description of a gentleman. It is in his lecture, *The Idea of a University,* ironical reading in a decade of "campus unrest.")

The duty of prayer is a key to such behavior. A Christian who obeys sincerely the behest to pray for "those in positions of responsibility," will exercise his vote with reason and regard for all, without the loud words and brash utterance which form the climate for violence, and with sympathy for harassed public men. Spend a minute relating this verse to your conduct as a citizen, at and between election years. The word occurs again in 3:4 ("gravity") and 3:8, 11 ("grave"). It is a word out of fashion in our noisy, impatient age of extreme opinions, loud-mouthed prejudice and exhibitionist conduct. But we would do well to resurrect the quality.

Observe that this regal quality is one for which we must pray. Paul hoped to see another type of man emerge, with all that was best in Roman, Greek and Jew, fused in a dignified Christlikeness. (See E. M. Blaiklock, *The Way of Excellence* [Pickering & Inglis] on that neglected study, Christian ethics.) Christianity manifests itself in our bearing, decorum, self-control, compassion — and the score of other godly qualities which mark the Christian citizen (see Phil. 1:27 and 3:20 in Berkeley, Goodspeed and Phillips).

3. *Verse 3*

The sense is: "Prayer for all men commends itself to the common conscience, and, a matter which is not surprising, accords with the will of God."

4. *Verse 4*

See Titus 2:11, and Psalm 97:2. Paul's vision of a global Gospel was embedded in the Old Testament (Extract illustrative verses from Psalms 95 to 100 and from the later prophecies of Isaiah). God is potentially "the Saviour of all men," but actually "of those who believe" (1 Tim. 4:10). Note that Paul does not say "wants to save," but "wants to be saved" ("whose will it is that all men should find salvation" NEB). Room is left for the reception or rejection of the proffered grace. "Knowledge of the truth" naturally follows the acceptance of salvation. The Lord laid down the principle (John 7:17). The word "truth" occurs fourteen times in the pastoral epistles (1 Tim. 3:15; 4:3; 6:5; 2 Tim. 2:15, 18; 3:8; 4:4; Titus 1:14). John picked up this thread in his theology.

5. *Verse 5*

The emphatic reference to "one God" may have pointed to some infiltration of pagan ideas in Ephesus. It was commonly believed that there were many saviors. Further, the logic is sound. It is possible for "all men" to have opportunity, if there is one God over all.

6. *Verse 6*

A fine expression of the Christology on which Paul has embarked in verse 5. It is the thought of Hebrew 4:15 and

NEB brings it out well: ". . . one mediator between God and *men,* Christ Jesus, himself *man,* who sacrificed himself to win freedom for all *mankind.* . . ."

7. *Verse 7*

Christianity involves preaching and teaching. This does not preclude or prevent "involvement" in society. No church program can afford to forget the pulpit ministry of preaching and teaching (*kerugma* and *didache*) and, if this is sound in content, and complete in its compass and appeal, social action, properly based and effectively ordered, will follow. The reverse process will not work. A certain revulsion from the preaching ministry today is no more than the reaction of those with nothing left to preach.

8. *Verses 8 to 15*

In view of the social situation at Ephesus (it was not unlike that of Corinth, another center of a fertility-cult built around the worship of a goddess) Paul firmly confined the public ministry of prayer to men.

To "lift the hands" was customary (1 Kings 8:22; Ps. 28:2; etc.), but more important than gesture is the state of mind and heart. No irritated (Matt. 6:14, 15; Mark 11:25) spirit or carping attitude ("excluding angry or quarrelsome thoughts" NEB) can promote prayer. Observe the searching phrases with which the model of all prayers, the Lord's prayer, opens.

Paul's directions to women may be left to make their own impact. Someone has said: "We must interpret the faith to the twentieth century, but not adjust to it. The century must adjust to the faith." The passage should be read in Phillips and NEB. The argument from Genesis on which he bases his conclusions may have greater force in a Jewish than a Gentile context, but the apostle's directions must be carefully pondered.

The *Expositor's Greek Testament* has an ingenious note: "Eve's reasoning faculty was overcome by the allegation of jealousy felt by God, an allegation plausible to a nature swayed by emotion rather than by reflection. The Tempter's statement seemed to be supported by the appearance of the fruit, as it was rendered attractive by hopes of vanity to be gratified. Adam's better judgment was overcome by personal influence (Gen. 3:17), he was not deceived. But the intellectual superior who sins against light may be morally inferior to him who stumbles in the dusk." Material surely for a warm debate in any study group! From the safety of the Antipodes the author of these study notes passes it on.

The difficult phrase, "she shall be saved in childbearing," remains. It is just possible that this could mean: "She shall be saved by the Childbearing" — a reference to Mary's gift of Christ and the words of Genesis 3:15, a chapter fresh in Paul's mind as he wrote. Montgomery's translation, following RV, supports this. The simpler explanation is better — the thought that woman's noblest and finest fulfillment is motherhood and all that it implies. In the carrying out of this function she escapes much of the stress of temptation, the drag of society and its corruption, and the wear and damaging burden of public life.

QUESTIONS FOR DISCUSSION

(i) Should we still pray for those in power?

(ii) What aspects of prayer are covered in the Lord's Prayer?

(iii) How does preaching differ from teaching?

(iv) What is the Christian basis for social action and in-involvement? What are the limits?

(v) What are the prerequisites of prayer? How should one prepare for prayer?

IV

CHAPTER THREE (1-15)

Introduction and Summary

The historical situation here is interesting. Timothy ministered in an area where the Church was strong and well-established. Titus was located in a more primitive community. Hence certain differences in the qualifications given for church leaders in the two epistles (see Titus 1). *NOTE:* 1. The possible distinction between bishops and elders remains a theme of controversy. It is likely that the two offices are identical, or that, in various sections of the church, divisions of labor and definitions of office varied. Church organization was patterned after social organization, and, in the Roman imperial order, there was considerable variety. One of the marks of exactitude in Luke is the precision with which he varies the names of Roman officials, in accord with local usage.

2. No late dating of the epistle can be based on the maturity of organization it describes. The social and political patterns of the Graeco-Roman world were well-developed and instinctive in city states. Any community would rapidly and efficiently order its plan of rule and leadership.

3. Paul obviously believed in the leadership of character. In organizing the church he was eager to see its conduct in the hands of good, sane, upright men. One denomination may differ from another today in its interpretation of church rule and government, but on one point all must be agreed — that those who presume to control "the

Body of Christ" must bring to that task demonstrable and proved qualities of moral leadership. They must first establish their call to rule others in Christ by governing well and firmly the common instincts and desires of their own persons, and the smaller community of their own families. That which is called for in the leaders of the church is equally demanded in the rank and file. In setting forth for Timothy the moral qualities requisite in bishop and deacon, Paul simply lists the qualities which every Christian might be expected to exhibit. None, therefore, is exempt from the impact and challenge of this chapter. Its rules still apply, and a more careful study of them would sometimes preserve a Christian community from all too common disruptions.

(Barclay's analysis of the chapter against its ancient historical background will repay careful reading. See also articles on "bishop," "deacon," and "elder" in PBD and other works of reference.)

Turning now to the text:

1. *Verses 1 to 3*

Paul begins by commending a laudable aspiration: to serve the church as leader and teacher, for the "bishop," "overseer" or "elder" served the community in both these capacities. The daunting list of qualities demanded of the aspirant for church leadership is enough to purge the poisoning pride out of all desire for leadership.

Consider now the qualities set forth as the ideal equipment for the Christian leader (vv. 2, 3).

1. *Blameless:* Phillips renders this "of blameless reputation"; Knox has it, "one with whom no fault can be found." It means "one against whom no charge can be levelled." "Which of you can convict me of wrongdoing?" asked the Lord of His foes (John 8:48). No man can issue such a challenge without the certainty of a prompt response, but the words of Paul point to a Christlikeness required of the aspirant to leadership. The only other contexts in which this word appears are 5:7 and 6:14.

"The husband of one wife" must be taken with "blamelessness," because it is in the area of sex or marital relations that visible causes of reproach were most likely to be found. Literally the words run "the man of one woman." Several meanings have been suggested: (a) Polygamy is forbidden. Although polygamy, according to Josephus, was not unknown among first-century Jews, Christians certainly never countenanced it. However, 5:9, which reverses the phrase, rules out this interpretation. (b) Concubinage, or any form of marital infidelity, is ruled out. (c) Celibacy is forbidden. But this interpretation is inconsistent with 1 Corinthians 7:17. (d) Second marriage (after the death of the first partner), elsewhere permitted (1 Cor. 7:39) or recommended (1 Tim. 5:14), is not allowable for a man who must appear beyond all reproach. The dominant idea is monogamous fidelity. These suggestions stand open for debate.

2. *Vigilant:* With a not uncommon inconsistency, the KJV renders the same word "sober" in v. 11 and Titus 2:2. Most versions agree on "temperate." Compare v. 8 and Titus 1:8, where another word of similar significance is used, and v. 3 where the word has the wider nuance of "quarrelsomeness over wine." The ASV is almost justified in its translation of "no brawler." The KJV is certainly wrong.

3. *Sober:* This is one of the most difficult words in Greek to render accurately. It suggests the goodness which avoids all extremes, a quality which the Greeks cherished. Romans 12:3 makes play with the corresponding verb. The word has two contributing roots, an adjective meaning "safe," and a noun meaning "mind." The notion in Greek was an ideal balance of thought which never moved to extremes. There is much truth and worth in the idea. Courage stands balanced between the vice of cowardice and the vice of rashness. Moral purity preserves a balance between impurity and prudery. Virtue is always delicately poised. If it slips either way, it gravitates to vice, it errs either by excess or defect. Observe, then, how inadequate a translation "sober" or "temperate" is. "Self-controlled" approaches it. "A man of balanced virtue" is nearer the mark.

4. *Well-behaved:* ("of good behavior," KJV): Other versions say "orderly," "dignified" — a quality which orderly behavior breeds. It is a fruit of 3, of "balanced virtue," a basic condition of 1. Paul comes back to the same sturdiness of character from a number of angles.

5. *Given to hospitality:* This is a necessary quality in a century when inns were dangerous, and places of immorality (5:10; Rom. 12:13; Heb. 13:2, 1 Pet. 4:9; 3 John 5). Note that the Greek word means "loving strangers."

6. *Apt to teach:* See also 2 Timothy 2:24; Titus 1:9; Ephesians 4:11. The deacon's task is passive (v. 9), the bishop's is active. Is there enough clear teaching today? What have we to teach? Here is a theme for study: the necessity, scope, effect, process and pattern of teaching.

7. *No striker:* This is allied to the first quality, see 3. Pugnacity, violence or combativeness are inconsistent with the qualities of 1, 3 and 4. But Paul probably has the treatment of slaves in mind. No man given to using a fist or stick on servants was worthy of Christian office. We can take the next two qualities along with this: "But patient, not a brawler" says the ASV. "Forbearing" is perhaps the best word (Phil. 4:5; Titus 3:2). Such a man is not greedy for the last penny to which he is entitled, not prone to swift retaliation, just as he is not ready with fist or weapon. He is not the duelling snob, the arrogant bully or the quick avenger.

8. *Not covetous:* The word simply says: "Not fond of money." Of course, the man who is not dollar-hungry cuts at the root many of the temptations which lead to the violent faults of 7. Also see 6:10. Paul thus lists the qualities of character needed by a leader. He then goes on to discuss the reputation a leader's family should have if he is not to cast aspersion on the church.

2. *Verses 4 and 5*

If a man's character or conduct is such that his own household is out of his control, and his children rebel, he has no right to presume to leadership in the wider family of the church, where the same faults or defects of personality, whether culpable, inborn or even innocent, will no doubt produce the same spectacle of revolt or lack of discipline.

The final phrase of verse 4 is variously rendered "with dignity, decorum, control." See 2:11. It does suggest a duty for Christian young people. A parent's testimony, usefulness, indeed qualification for office, can be called into question by exhibitionism, expressed in disrespect, unbecoming behavior, and lack of discipline by his child.

The Church is a household (1 Cor. 4:1; Gal. 6:10; Eph. 3:9; Num. 12:7; Hos. 8:1). See Luke 16:10 for the whole notion. "Take care of" — the verb of the Good Samaritan is used twice in Luke 10:34-35, the only other instances of its use in the New Testament.

3. *Verses 6 and 7*

The parallel passage in Titus, which shows a similar structure of leadership and organization in Crete, a younger and less educationally endowed community, significantly omits anything corresponding to these verses. The word "novice" means "no new shoot" and in the Septuagint is used of newly planted trees (Ps. 144:12). The temptation to damaging pride would be less in a small despised community, greater in such a place as Ephesus, where the Christian group was becoming a recognized society.

The verb translated "lifted up with pride" occurs only here, and at 6:4 and 2 Timothy 3:4, but it is the vice of 1 Corinthians 13:4; "Love . . . is not swelled with conceit." See C. S. Lewis on pride, the fundamental sin (*Christian Behavior*) and *The Way of Excellence* (E. M. Blaiklock, Pickering & Inglis), pp. 22-24.

"Lest he come under the same condemnation as the devil." "By that sin fell the angels." Note how the beginning of verse 7 returns to "blameless" of v. 2. "Those without" know what to expect of a Christian. "The Canaanite and the Perizzite dwell in the land," as Abraham reminded Lot, when tension invaded their common camp. The message of a faulty church, as of a faulty Christian, is vitiated at the beginning. For the kindly phrase for non-Christians, "those not of the family," see 1 Corinthians 5:12; Colossians 4:5; 1 Thessalonians 4:12.

4. Verse 8

We return to detail with the list of demanding qualifications for "deacons," the lesser "serving-officers" of the Church. Those interested in the scope, nature and institution of this office, should look up the relevant articles in the Bible dictionaries. Our study is again an investigation of words.

1. *Grave.* This word (*semnos*), variously rendered "worthy of respect" (Amp.), "dignified" (Rhm), "of serious outlook" (JBP) or "of high principle" (NEB), was discussed above. The Roman "gravity," and the Stoic "reserve" are in the word. Such an attitude does not call for one "to pluck the thorn and throw away the rose," but it does demand a certain thoughtful avoidance of extremes, exhibitionism in dress or in demeanor, frivolity and extravagance of speech or conduct.

2. *Not double-tongued.* Within its context the word probably means the concern for communication, which, in the pure interests of truth, avoids the adaptation of speech or language according to the person being addressed, "saying one thing to one person, another to another," as Bengel paraphrases. "Deceitful or insincere in speech," says OED. This is not commendation of brutal frankness, nor criticism of the proper courtesies and proprieties of conversation and address. It forbids a form of falsehood.

3. The next two qualities — "not addicted to wine or greedy of base gain" — have already been dealt with.

5. Verses 9 to 13

Verse 9 suggests simplicity and sincerity of belief. "Mystery" was a familiar word in the vocabulary of ancient religion. It suggested those deeper truths revealed or apparent only to those accepted by the cult. In the Christian contexts of its use (Matt. 13:11; Eph. 1:9; Rom. 16:25; 1 Cor. 13:2), the word conveys the idea of that knowledge of

God, His ways, and the meaning of the Gospel, which come only after the committal of faith has been made. NEB renders it well: "These must be men who combine a clear conscience with a firm hold on the deep truths of our faith."

A clear conscience forbids all reservations in belief. Let the unsure, the doubleminded and the unconvinced be excluded from office. The Church must be led by men who believe every word they say. The tragedy of the 'sixties was the easy victory of a small band of iconoclasts won over churchmen of feeble faith — the Munich School of theologians, of Austin Farrer's phrase, always ready to sell the pass, in the weak belief that they can stop somewhere in the foothills, people talked easily out of all firm conviction, and too busy learning from their enemies to be of any use to those who hoped to be their friends. No one should function, in pulpit or officer's chair, save men of sturdy faith, and mastering conviction. Hence the proving demanded in verse 10.

Hence, also, the involvement of their wives (v. 11), for a deacon can be disqualified or embarrassed in office by a marriage partner who is not "a woman of discretion and self-control — who can be trusted" (JBP). The deacon's home and household, in fact, like that of his superiors in office, must demonstrate his ability to guide and to command respect (vv. 11, 12).

Verse 11 may possibly refer to deaconesses, not the wives of deacons. It simply says in the Greek text: "Likewise must women be . . ." Pliny, writing to Trajan from Bithynia in A.D. 110, to describe the Christian Church in his province which was under investigation, mentions two deaconesses examined by his officers (*Epistles* 10:97). Phoebe (Rom. 16:1) was no doubt such a leader.

Verse 13 concludes on the same note with which the chapter began: "Those who have served well as deacons, have won for themselves high standing, and the right to speak openly on the Christian faith" (mostly NEB). Properly held by the right people, such a privilege is a fair reward, and one to be humbly sought.

6. *Verses 14 to 16*

In conclusion, says Paul, here are general guidelines by which you can organize the household of faith. Hold fast to the ethical standards, and details will fall into place. It is a precious thing you handle, and to be reverently approached. After all, he concludes, it is the church which is committed to your care, "a pillar and foundation of the truth." Note the indefinite article. Christ is the Truth; the Gospel is its relevant expression; the church one of its supports.

This epistle was first read in Ephesus, where the mighty temple of Artemis, one of the wonders of the world, stood. Some of its pillars of green marbled stone may be seen today in St. Sophia in Istanbul. In Paul's day they stood in polished beauty, and provided the vast foundations which such a building demanded. No man of Ephesus could read Paul's word without thinking of this shrine.

In verse 16 Paul ends with what may have been one of the doctrinal antiphonal chants by which the church, before the whole New Testament was in its hands, propagated and established doctrine. Pliny, the governor of Bithynia in A.D. 110, told how his investigators found that the Christians, at their dawn meeting, sang alternately a hymn to Christ as God. This may have been part of the hymn. Its alternation is between earthly and heavenly, and its theme the Incarnation and its authentication. Consider John 1:31, 2:28, 33:2, 21:1, 14; Romans 16:26; Colossians 1:26, 3:4, 4:23; 2 Timothy 1:10; Titus 1:3; 1 Peter 1:20, 5:4; 1 John 1:2, 3:5, 8.

QUESTIONS FOR DISCUSSION
    (i) What are the qualities required in a leader?
  (ii) Does the organization of the early church justify varieties of organization in the Church today?
 (iii) Do titles matter?
 (iv) Ambition, good and bad.
  (v) The Christian view of second marriage.
 (vi) Balance, moderation, and extremes, in the moral sphere.

(vii) Hospitality as a Christian virtue. How is it used?

(viii) The absoluteness of Christian standards.

(ix) The Christian and violence.

(x) Discipline in a household. What is the Christian view of discipline?

(xi) The part of the family in a parent's testimony.

(xii) Dignity. Its worth and its abuse.

(xiii) Honesty, courtesy, and frankness in speech. What of the so-called "frank friend"?

V

CHAPTER FOUR (1-16)

Introduction and Summary

Paul's absolute emancipation from all legalism is apparent in this chapter. Knowing men, he foresees that there will arise those who will corrupt the simplicity of the Gospel, pervert its preaching to personal advantage, burden it with human traditions, rules, and prohibitions, thus making doctrine irrelevant to life and difficult. There is always heresy where man or system intervenes between the sinner and his Mediator (v. 5). When religion anywhere becomes complicated and hard to understand, it may generally be set down as human tampering with matters of the Spirit. The Lord's doctrine was clear, practical, and close to the need and thinking of the common folk who, we are told, "heard him gladly." Paul, casting aside the Pharisaic legal system in which he spent half his life, was like his Lord — plain, sane, and potent. Such a minister he desired Timothy to be, and the noble words have come down the centuries with encouragement for all young men who have sought the Christian ministry. Let them offset their inexperience with their mode of living and their manifest uprightness of character (12), and let them serve after the manner of their gifts (14), think as well as act, and live devotedly (15), keeping the Gospel pure (16).

1. Verses 1 to 3

All the writers of the New Testament epistles speak of the rise of heretical teaching. Glance through the epistles of Peter, Jude and John. The Church had survived the attempt to turn it into a sect of reformed Judaism. The epistle to the Galatians is the major document of that clash. The first of the letters to Corinth shows the beginnings of the second peril, the attempt sharply visible in the letters of John and in Revelation 2 and 3, to work out a compromise with paganism (see "Nicolaitan" and "Cerinthus" in Bible dictionaries). The "heathen" are always returning to the attack, and those interested in the somber pageant of conflict will find an interesting evening's reading in G. K. Chesterton's magnificent poem, *The Ballad of the White Horse.*

Neither this passage, nor its parallels justify such misguided attempts as those of Albert Schweitzer to interpret the New Testament on eschatological principles.

"The latter times" are not necessarily the end of the age. The translators say: "in later times" (ASV), "in after times" (NEB), "in later days" (Knox). It is well to remember in all such contexts that we deal with an intrusion of eternity into time, and that a constant awareness and vigilance are called for.

Paul claims specific guidance from God in this matter. He was always acutely aware of the peril of hypocrisy and apostasy, and it is curious to find the two spiritual faults bracketed (v. 2). "Double-talk," which, when it becomes a fixed habit, incurs the judgment of self-deception by becoming "double-think," is a prime example, and an intruding phenomenon in some modern preaching. Verse 2 is a "searing" (KJV) indictment of this species of dishonesty. NEB says ". . . the specious falsehoods of men whose own conscience is branded with the devil's sign." And Phillips, with his customary vigor, says: ". . . teachings given by men who are lying hypocrites, whose consciences are as dead as seared flesh."

Paul is clear that such apostasy is organized by a malign intelligence (v. 1), finding tools and agents in those who have resisted the Holy Spirit's persuasion firmly and consciously enough to incur the judgment of insensitivity. See Ephesians 6:12 ff.

(Relevant themes for study emerge: 1. *Apostasy* in the pastoral epistles and the epistles of Peter and John. 2. *Paul's charge* to the Ephesian elders (Acts 20), then the nature of apostasy as seen in the apocalyptic picture of the Ephesian church in Revelation 2. 3. *The hardened conscience* in the Lord's warning to the Pharisees, who had proceeded to the willful blindness which turns good into evil (Mark 3). Consider "the unpardonable sin" (see E. M. Blaiklock, *In The Image of Peter* [Moody Press], chapter 2).

Paul marks certain ascetic practices as the sign of the dissident group he has in immediate view. (*The Oxford Dictionary of the Christian Church* carries two articles on asceticism and celibacy, with full references for those disposed to carry this study further.) The obscure heresy dealt with in the letter to Colossae mentions certain taboos in food (Col. 2:16). Romans 14 suggests similar false emphases in other churches. The Levitical law had been precise in such matters; the practice of such groups of ascetics as the Essenes had made much of certain abstinences. Pagan challenges, as the first epistle to Corinth shows, were a problem for Christians.

It was difficult to steer a sane and uncluttered course. It still is. Here are some guidelines for discussion: 1. Christ called for self-denial (Mark 8:34, 9:29; Luke 9:57-62); Paul counsels the same ideas (Rom. 8:13; 1 Cor. 9:25 ff; Col. 3:5). How does this fit with vv. 4 and 5, with "the Son of Man who came eating and drinking," in contrast with the disciples both of John and of the Pharisees? 2. Compare the Corinthian situation (1 Cor. 8) with the modern need for Christian abstinence. Chart a plain course for Christians. 3. Is marriage ever inadvisable or wrong? What other views did Paul have?

2. *Verses 4 and 5*

These verses have been anticipated in their general sense before, but they require some special remarks. Note that v. 4 loosely paraphrased reads: "Everything that God has made is of absolute worth, and not to be rejected if it can be received with thanksgiving." See Revelation 14:14; 1 Corinthians 8:8-12; Titus 1:15. The decisive question is: Viewing this thing in the light of health, social impact, my testimony, the "weaker brother," responsible stewardship, and my family — is it such that I can without incongruity ask God's blessing on my consumption or use of it? Does it measure up to the two points in the verse, that is, "made by God," and "received with thanksgiving"?

Verse 5 enlarges this meaning. That which is of God is a holy thing and acknowledged as such, by a prayer which is in accord with God's revealed will in His word. Look at First Corinthians 10:31-32, then Acts 27:35. ". . . it is consecrated by prayer and by the Scripture used in it" Goodspeed).

3. Verses 6 to 16

Here is the commission from a mighty leader of the Church to the next generation. This is the call to witness, and none are exempt from that call. All must be ready to teach and to preach, in one form or another. Seventy-six generations have gone by, but the charge is still relevant. Nineteen centuries ago, in A.D. 69, Paul had been dead perhaps two years. This was "the year of the four emperors," when, on Nero's sordid death, the ends of the earth marched on Rome, and the army groups on the military frontiers set up their own commanders as emperors and fought a multilateral civil war in Italy. The long horror of the Jewish Rebellion was moving to its sanguinary close when Vespasian, who was in command in Palestine, became emperor. It was the year when "the Beast," as was quoted above, was almost destroyed, but was "healed of his deadly wound; and all the world wondered" (Rev. 13:3). In the seventies of the twentieth century these are still relevant.

Glance at each verse in sequence.

A. Verse 6. "In setting these matters before the brethren, you will be a good servant of Christ Jesus, ever nourishing yourself on the words of the faith, and the good doctrine which you have followed." So, literally rendered, the verse runs. There is food for the soul in the pure teaching of Christianity. Observe the importance of doctrine, and mark the implication that weakness in church, personal life, and testimony follows the combination, attenuation, corruption or abandonment of "good doctrine." Doctrine is also something taught (Latin: *doctrina*; Greek: *didaskalia*). (Consider this, and focus the thought on congregations and ministers of your acquaintance.)

B. Verse 7. "Turn away from the babbling of old women, and exercise yourself rather for godliness." This use of "exercise" is obscure. Perhaps some foolish female member of the church, or in Timothy's circle, was preaching some form of asceticism, some "exercise" of spirit. Many parts of Paul's letters would be clearer, if we had the letters written to him, which he was often answering, or if we had closer acquaintance with the existing situation. Perhaps the adjective was only one of contempt. At any rate, some nonsense was abroad inimical to "good doctrine." Paul, with characteristic vehemence, says that, if Christianity demands certain "exercise," it can find all it needs in practicing godliness, or in training for it like a Greek athlete.

C. Verse 8. "For bodily exercise (Greek: *gymnasia*) has its minor usefulness, but godliness ('spiritual training,' as the Amplified Bible adds) is of all-round value, containing, as it does, the promise of life here and hereafter." Note: (1) Paul is not decrying physical fitness, or even an athlete's training; he concedes that these have a certain value; (2) he is extending the image: the body, however trained, dies, while the soul endures; (3) he widens the Christian's scope: this life is not all — which is his point in 1 Corinthians 15:19, and a truth to be contrasted with the secularism of the so-called "new" theology.

D. Verse 9 looks back. The "saying" is verse 8. See 1:15, in full. It seems a Pauline formula to underline and to emphasize a truth.

E. Verse 10. "For to this end we toil and struggle, because we have set our hope on the living God, who is the Savior of all men, and especially of those who believe."

Two most important points follow:

(i) Christianity is not easy. Consider the word-pictures. "We toil" — this is the word used in John 4:38 where the reference is to the farmer toiling in the winter-mud and cold so that a summer-harvest may be ready for others, perhaps, to reap. It also appears in Philippians 2:16 in the context of athletic toil and striving. Here Paul probably has in mind the same thought as in verses 7 and 8 which he continues with a second verb. The English "agonize" derives from it. "Agon" was the Greek for an athletic contest, and is used in Hebrews 12:1. A fairly well-attested variant provides the KJV reading "suffer reproach." Pause, at any rate, and consider the word-pictures in Scripture and hymnology about the difficult task before the Christian.

(ii) Does the conclusion of the verse favor Universalism? Remember that in Scripture and in the work of any writer, statement must be balanced by statement. Paul nowhere teaches that all men, whether accepting or rejecting Christ, are "saved" (This theme could be followed up in study). All he says is that God is potentially the Savior of all, for "none are cast out who come" (John 6:37). Of course, He is "especially" the Savior of those who "work out" the accepted salvation.

F. Verse 11. Parallel with verse 9. Observe the pattern in the exhortation. Both verses call for pause and consideration after an important statement. Observe, too, the note of authority: "Command and teach."

G. Verse 12. Authority? By a young man? Why not — provided that young man sets an example in (1) his speech — on all occasions; consider this in relation to social intercourse, conducting meetings, preaching; (2) conduct and manner of life, exemplified in the last three nouns — love, i.e., one's attitude of compassion, tolerance, and Christlikeness; faith, i.e., the sturdiness and steadfastness of one's convictions; purity, i.e., personal sanctity and command of self.

H. Verse 13. Parallels 9 and 11. Note the three tasks of the young church-leader (Timothy was probably in his early thirties): reading, preaching, studying. They cannot be dissociated.

I. Read the remaining three verses in NEB and Phillips, or some other modern translation. The "laying on of hands" was a symbolic transmission of authority inherited from Judaism (Deut. 34:9; Num. 8:10). The eldership were led to this act of endowment by "prophecy" — that is, by divine insight, accorded them either at Lystra (Acts 14:23) or on a later occasion (2 Tim. 1:6). Observe that the whole duty of witness depends, in Paul's view, on the quality of the teacher (involving quiet assessment of his enablement, and persistent self-discipline), and the soundness of his teaching.

QUESTIONS FOR DISCUSSION
   (i) The Christian's attitude towards heresy. How is the line drawn between legitimate difference of opinion, and destructive deviation?
  (ii) The Christian attitude toward alcohol.
 (iii) "Christianity is not easy."
 (iv) Authority in the Church! Who is qualified to hold it?
  (v) Preaching and study.
 (vi) The qualities of a good teacher. List them.

VI

CHAPTER FIVE (1-25)

Introduction and Summary

This chapter is pungently translated and well set out in Phillips' rendering. Paul sets out to deal with some of the social problems of the community of believers, and the position of widows was a pressing need. Paul lays down one or two rules for such charity, and they reveal both his sturdy common sense, and the difficulties of the situation with which Timothy was called to deal. First, says Paul, let a Christian remember that religion begins at home. Secondly, let the Church remember that widows who claim its aid should demonstrate their worthiness. They should have deserved well of their neighbors, and bear a good testimony in the community. Younger widows, in Paul's experience, speedily contemplate remarriage — an attitude which, in his view, contained an element of disloyalty. Let them remarry, and in so doing become less of a social burden. Paul was writing in a pagan world, as yet scarcely tinged with Christianity. Let Timothy also discipline the church, not be in a hurry to ordain officers of the church (22), and avoid the stomach troubles caused by the polluted water of the congested city, by using a little wine. It follows that, normally, Timothy abstained.

The structure of this chapter is casual, and its contents simple. Throughout Scripture God uses the common things of life to press home His message, and the New Testament letters are real letters, besides being the Word of God. That is why the simplicities and ordinariness of our own lives make a framework for our testimony and our usefulness.

But specifically two facts are to be noted in this connection: (1) it is part of anyone's familiar epistolary style to chat without careful order about common problems; (2) some of the difficulties (only minor ones) in these two chapters might be removed if we could but know the situation in Ephesus, or perhaps the problems raised in a communication of Timothy to Paul, which no longer exists.

Looking, then, synoptically at the whole chapter, we may raise some questions about its modern application, before proceeding to a detailed commentary. (Note how, in the four chapters already covered, approach, method of study, and analysis vary in each case.) The following themes emerge:

(1) the necessity for social work in the church community, and the consequent need for a structure of administration;

(2) whether with the growth of the "welfare state," "paternalism," and "social security," the need for social work within the Christian community is as great; is there still an area?

(3) the wider significance of mutual care, as a by-product of Christian love;

(4) the danger of ill-balance between "social" and "evangelical" Christianity; are they mutually exclusive? What of Moody, and the Salvation Army?

Proceeding to detail:

1. Verses 1 and 2

An "elder" here, as commentators and translators generally agree, is an older person (Weymouth, Moffatt; Phillips has "a senior member of your church"). Nothing so ill becomes the young as rudeness. Nothing will be more certainly requited, for the young inevitably become old. Consider: "There is no outward sign of true courtesy that does not rest on a deep moral foundation" (Goethe). "The grace of God is in courtesy" (Belloc).

Discourtesy toward age rises from contempt for the

tradition, and the times age represents. There is no clearer sign of ignorance and defective education.

Note: (1) no blind obedience is demanded, only a correct approach: "appeal to him as a father" (Goodspeed); (2) Paul's conception of the Church as a family lies behind both verses; (3) note the call for respect toward girls, and a propriety in friendliness.

2. *Verses 3 to 16*

Verse 3: "Honour" is possible, but probably the use is a more mundane one, sanctioned for this verb by several contexts. "Look after widows who are really dependent" (Goodspeed); "Widows in real need must be supported from the funds" (Moffatt); "honour" is a euphemism.

Verse 4: But observe that there are priorities in obligation. The community is not to be burdened when there are closer relatives more immediately exposed to the duty of support. In more spheres than finance, the home is the place where Christianity must find expression. Fail there, and a more public testimony is invalidated.

Verse 5: Paul sees in the helplessness and loneliness of widowhood a challenge to seek refuge in God, and to prayer. Is there a deep principle here involved, touching the problem of pain and suffering? See Luke 2:37.

Verse 6: Surely Paul refers to a specific case of wanton widowhood which Timothy has set before him. The Greek would allow this interpretation. Follow through with a concordance the notion of death in life (Rev. 3:1; Rom. 7:10, 24; Eph. 4:18).

Verse 7: Like 4:11 and 15, a pause to underline and emphasize. But here the pronoun suggests that Paul refers on, not back: "Add these orders to the rest" (NEB).

Verses 7 and 8: Like 4:11 and 15, the phrase "these things" indicates that a statement of some moment follows. The *Expositor's Greek Testament* remarks: "One of the most subtle temptations of the devil is that we can best comply with the demands of duty in some place far away from our home." Consider (1) Mark 5:18, 19; (2) "Beginning

at Jerusalem" . . . "The path of duty begins from within our
own house, and we must walk it on our own feet"; (3)
Christ Himself began His public ministry, it appears, only
when Mary's other children were of age; (4) duty is not
measured by human and statistical estimates of opportunity;
(5) Christian disregard for non-Christian standards of
morality or conduct invalidates all testimony; (6) proper
provision for the family is a first call on financial resources:
(7) Christian parents, who deprive their own children of
attention, care and company for alleged "Christian work,"
fail in their first sphere of duty. Can they succeed in the
second? "Press these facts upon them, so that they may live
lives free from reproach" (7, Weymouth).

Verse 9: Luke 8:3; Acts 9:36; Romans 16:1. These verses
point to a female ministry of sorts. There was a widows'
"list," which appears again in patristic writings. It seems
that widows who enjoyed communal support had some
social obligations laid upon them in return for the benefits
received. A social principle may be involved.

Verse 10: "It is characteristic of the sanity of apostolic
Christianity that, as typical examples of 'good works,' Paul
instances the discharge of commonplace duties" (EGT).
Note (1) not necessarily for her own children; orphans were
a group in the early church; (2) "hospitality is a virtue
especially demanded in a condition of society in which there
is much going to and fro . . ." (EGT); consider this in a
modern context; (3) "washing the feet" was a symbol of
humble service (1 Sam. 25:41; Luke 7:38; John 13:14).

Verse 11: Young widows are not, it may be supposed,
excluded from relief. They are not to be listed permanently
because they may remarry, and also they constitute a major
risk of scandal.

Verse 12: ". . . incurring condemnation" (*New American Standard Bible*) . . . "censure" (Weymouth). Widows
were free to remarry (1 Cor. 7:39). Read: "because they
have made void their first pledge", i.e., the undertaking
made when being listed as widows? Hence the direction
not so to enroll the younger women? Perhaps the Ephesian

church had run into difficulties here? If we had Timothy's report we should know.

Verse 13: Besides, such situations of security make the younger women idle gossips. Paul's personality peeps out. He had small patience with frivolous and talkative women.

Verse 14: Hence a plain direction to marry again, and perform a proper function. The "adversary" was any ready critic of the church (1 Cor. 16:9; Phil. 1:28) . . . "and so avoid giving the enemy any opportunity for scandal" (*Twentieth Century New Testament*); . . . "any excuse for abusing us" (Goodspeed); . . . "no handle for speaking ill of us" (Knox). Note this salutary care for the honor of the church.

Verse 15: Some reason, at Ephesus or in Paul's wider experience, lent urgency to the advice of verse 16.

Verse 16: Almost certainly the verse is to be explained by a specific question referred by Timothy. To give ruling by letter was a common judicial process in the Roman system. The imperial replies were called "rescripts." Hence Vol. X of Pliny's correspondence, with requests for Trajan's rulings about the Christians, and many other details of administrative difficulty, which Pliny encountered in the administration of Bithynia, in A.D. 110-112. Paul writes here like an emperor giving a decision to a case in point: "Any Christian woman who has widowed relatives, should look after them. . . . The church can look after widows who are really dependent" (Goodspeed).

3. *Verses 17 to 25*

Paul's direction over the care and proper financial support for widows reminds him of another subject not without connection. Let "elders be properly supported." With plain common sense, he suggests that the remuneration should be in proportion to the service rendered.

All elders (17) were not engaged in preaching and teaching, as well as in the tasks of administration associated with their office. First Corinthians 12, where Paul develops the metaphor of the body, is clear illustration that, generally speaking, Paul did not expect a many-sided activity among the rulers of the community. But those able to exercise a dual role were worthy of recognition. The literal force of "double" need not be pressed, but "honour" means more than respectful regard. It obviously contains the notion of an "honorarium" for those devoting their full time, or significant amounts of it to active service.

An elder, on the other hand, who failed in his duty (19), or was alleged so to fail, was at least entitled to such equity of trial as one accused under the Law (Deut. 19:15). On proof of shortcoming, exposure and rebuke must be public, and impartial (20, 21).

Verse 22 is difficult. It may mean: (i) Do not rush a man into office until his fitness for it has been tried and tested. This would rule out recent converts (NEB, Moffatt, Taylor); (ii) Do not discharge a repentant delinquent until his sorrow for his sin has been truly made manifest. There appears to have been a practice to receive a penitent back into full fellowship by a ritual of "laying on of hands." Either (i) or (ii) gives a meaning to the closing clause. Knox renders it well: ". . . and so share the blame for the sins of others." (i) is the much more likely interpretation.

Verse 23 touches on Paul's anxiety for the moral health of a young man in a city which flaunted sexual vice. In more ways than one, the twentieth is more like the first than any of those that lie between. The advice to drink "a little wine" is to be seen in context. A pure water supply was unknown in most large cities. Where it was possible, as in Rome, to drink piped water, the erosion from the lead piping was no doubt responsible for a greater or less degree of lead poisoning. At any rate in this alcohol-ridden age, with crime and death on the road lifted shockingly by social drinking, there is no mandate here for anything other than Christian abstinence. The last verse of First Corinthians 8 is surely decisive. And, as we have remarked, it also follows that normally Timothy did not take wine.

The last two verses, abruptly closing the section, surely refer to a statement of Timothy, expressing hesitation over the moral judgments he was called upon to make in his post of responsibility at Ephesus. There is a loose connection: Paul is anxious over (i) Timothy's moral integrity in the evil city; (ii) his physical health and his chronic dyspepsia — perhaps a sign of strain in his office; (iii) his decisiveness in ruling the church community, and his diagnosis of sin and virtue — the former for rebuke, the latter for promotion.

QUESTIONS FOR DISCUSSION

(i) Consider the four themes on the social significance of the Gospel set out in the closing paragraph of the Introduction to this chapter on page 54.

(ii) "The grace of God is in courtesy" (Belloc).

(iii) Duty. How is it measured, and where is it found?

(iv) Gossip, conversation and calumny in the church.

(v) Suitability for office in new converts.

(vi) Christian morality in a pagan environment. What should be our attitude to a corrupt movie industry, a debased TV program, and other expressions of a non-Christian society?

VII

CHAPTER SIX (1-21)

Introduction and Summary

Some have wondered that Christianity did not forthwith condemn the evil institution of slavery ("servants" in v. 1 is "slaves"). It is part of God's plan to work through the free will of man, and the unformed conscience of the age was not yet ready willingly to abandon an ancient system on which the structure of society depended. Christianity contained that which ultimately destroyed slavery. When men are equal before God, and Christ died for all, both bond and free, it is obvious that no man in Christ can lawfully hold possession of the person of another. Christianity killed slavery by exposing its evil roots, but only when the conscience of men was alive to the sin. A law of the Holy Spirit's action is herein illustrated. God leads His people to increasing enlightenment. He who seeks in prayer, and in sincerity, for the will of God, is aware of a sharpening of conscience, of a deepening dissatisfaction with past performance, and an ever increasing pressure on reluctant sin. God's blessing is not withdrawn from those who stumble amid faith's first difficulties, nor is one's attainment always matched by another's. The onward striving is what God demands, the forgetting of things behind, and the pressing on to the prize of the upward calling.

This is a chapter, then, apart from this major issue, of mingled final words and directions from which two or three main themes emerge: (1) the church and slavery; (2) the spiritual implications of affluence; (3) the need for a clear, sane testimony. Substitute race relations for the first, and observe how modern the chapter is.

1. *Verses 1 and 2*

Two quotations, as a basis for discussion or consideration:

1. "From contemporary literature, notably Seneca, who was writing at the same time, it is possible to show that enlightened minds, especially those in touch with Stoicism, were beginning to reject the old doctrine of Aristotle that some were born to slavery. . . . Slavery was meeting its first faint challenge. Why did not the Church take a lead, and its greatest spokesman take this occasion (the letter to Philemon) to speak out?

"Because Paul's message was not a social gospel. Because the social benefits of the faith were by-products which could flow effectively only from men transformed. Because vast reforms cannot safely be imposed from above, but must rise from below, rooted in the conscious consent of men. Because society, bound economically to slavery, would have lapsed into chaos at a sudden change, and collapse, bloodshed, and revolution were not part of the preaching of peace. Because it would have been folly to challenge the State in a manner which could only have brought reprisal, repression, and defeat. Because the Christian doctrine of the love of God, and the value of the human personality, cut slavery at the root, and ensured the ultimate withering away.

"So Paul, in his wisdom, sent Onesimus home. He sent him, nevertheless, with his human worth underlined. He was no 'speaking tool,' in the ancient phrase, no 'living instrument,' 'a personal chattel,' but a son, a brother in Christ. . . ." (*From Prison in Rome*, by E. M. Blaiklock, pp. 65, 66).

2. "The politico-social problem of the first ages of Christianity was the relation of free men to slaves, just as the corresponding problem before the Church in our own day is the relation of the white to the colored races. The grand truth of the brotherhood of man is the revolutionary fire

which Christ came to set. Fire, if it is to minister to civilization, must be so controlled as to be directed. So with the social ethics of Christianity; the extent to which their logical consequences are pressed must be calculated by common sense. One of the great dangers to the interests of the Church in early times was the teaching of the gospel on liberty and equality, crude and unqualified by consideration of other natural social conditions, also divinely ordered, which Christianity was called to leaven, not wholly to displace" (*Expositor's Greek Testament*, IV, 139.).

2. *Verses 3 to 6*

Paul's guiding motive in directing as he did on slavery was that the Christian teaching "should not be brought into disrepute" (NEB). There was, however, many a "pompous ignoramus" (4, NEB) in the church who presumed in Paul's day to contradict; people filled with "a morbid appetite for discussions and arguments" (Williams); "quibbling over the meaning of Christ's words and stirring up arguments" (Taylor.) The result? "Defamations, quarrelings, wrangling, ill-natured suspicions, recriminations, malicious innuendoes, abusive language, perpetual contention, constant friction, mutual irritation, minds warped . . ." The list is collected from five translations of verses 4-5, checked against the original. Note the metaphor of health in verses 3-4: "wholesome" and "morbidly preoccupied" (KJV "doting").

Questions arising: (1) unhealthiness of controversy; (2) the condition of the early Church (compare the Corinthian church, and the glimpse of Timothy's Ephesian church, with its Nicolaitan minority, in Rev. 2); in fact, we speak with considerable looseness of the "early Church." One commentator remarks: "To think of getting back to its life is simply to talk of what we do not understand. Paul's great endeavor, his mighty struggle and incessant prayer, was to get it away from its own feeble life, to lift it to a higher level and a purer air." (3) The vital importance of sound doctrine and authority. Are all matters open to dispute? (4) Sources of tension in the Church.

3. Verses 6 to 10

Why Paul reverts to riches and their snare is not clear. Perhaps those who questioned sound doctrine in the Ephesian church were the emerging Nicolaitans, rejected later (Rev. 2:6), who sought some form of compromise with pagan society. It was upon the rich (e.g. in Laodicea) that the temptation to compromise came most insistently.

"Contentment" inadequately renders *autarkeia*. Paul uses the cognate adjective *autarkes* at Philippians 4:11. It was a word which was a favorite with the Stoics. The Stoics taught that their "wise man" was indifferent to material things. He must dominate self and live above circumstances. The Stoic's proud scorn for all that men could do to his person or his possessions produced many a story of grim endurance in the face of tyranny, pain and loss. His head was ever unbowed, bloodied though it be. But in the struggle to achieve such self-sufficiency, the Stoic crushed all emotion and hardened his heart. As T. R. Glover put it, adapting a phrase of Tacitus, he "made a desert of the heart and called it peace." The Epicureans, the other great philosophic school, found *autarkeia* in renunciation. The Epicureans narrowed ambition and desire. They taught the littleness of all the objects of man's passionate strife, the futility, indeed, of all striving.

"The Christian can follow neither Epicurean nor Stoic. The Lord's own death was not the proud, defiant, wordless death of the Stoic. Nor was He withdrawn, hard, aloof. The Christian is involved in life. He must feel, and feel more acutely than the selfish escapist. He is not disillusioned, cynical, contemptuous. The Christian is 'self-sufficient,' for thus *autarkes* is literally rendered, because he is 'in Christ,' and Christ is God, and God is all-sufficient. Paul's *autarkeia* lay in the knowledge that God has not lost control, that circumstances are either of His devising, or of His permissive will" (*From Prison in Rome*, by E. M. Blaiklock, p. 55). Render, then: ". . . and, of course, religion does yield high dividends, but only to the man whose resources are within him" — that is, Christ within is the Christian's "self-sufficiency."

". . . but those who keep scheming to get rich expose themselves to temptation, and lay themselves open to all sorts of silly and wicked desires." (9) In other words, there is no harm in wealth, but the process of getting wealth is a spiritually perilous one.

This leads to the second comment, the oft-quoted verse 10. The literal meaning is rather, as Knox renders: "For the love of money is a root from which every kind of evil springs." Here is Phillips on the whole verse: "For loving money leads to all kinds of evil, and some men in the struggle to be rich have lost their faith and caused themselves untold agonies of mind." This makes the meaning clear.

4. *Verses 11 to 16*

Now the epilogue. Several comments: (1) "O man of God" is a most honorable vocative. It was the Old Testament term for prophet (1 Sam. 9:6; 1 Kings 12:22; 13:1), and the most moving of compliments to the young man in Ephesus.

(2) "Constantly strive for righteousness" (cf. Prov. 15:9; Rom. 9:30; 2 Tim. 2:22). This is defined as justice, godliness, fidelity and love. (Follow each with a concordance — Zondervan has published an "expanded concordance" covering five versions of the Bible.)

(3) Follow through Paul's metaphor of the games — the "good fight" refers to gymnastic rather than military conflict. Again, see concordance (1 Cor. 9:24; Phil. 3:12, 14; 2 Tim. 4:7). "Lay hold of eternal life" expands the imagery. This is the crown (James 1:12; Rev. 2:10).

(4) Jesus is the Faithful Witness (John 18:37; Rev. 1:5). Note Paul's implicit confirmation of the story of the trial as given in the fourth gospel. It was already firmly based in the oral tradition of the church.

(5) The "appearing" of verse 14 is *epiphaneia,* anglicized as "epiphany." Here of the Second Coming, elsewhere called the *parousia* (1 Cor. 15:23; 1 Thess. 2:19; 3:13; 4:15; 5:23; 2 Thess. 2:1). "In His times" shows Paul's acceptance of the fact that Christ's second coming cannot be dated.

(6) Linger over this magnificent doxology, and read it in other versions.

5. *Verses 17 to 21*

This conclusion is in two parts: (1) A further charge to the rich at Ephesus. There must have been a problem of some seriousness among the well-to-do of the Christian community in the great city. Paul approaches the theme in the traditional fashion. "Treasures laid up in heaven" are the only riches worthwhile. The reference to the Sermon on the Mount is clear. Matthew's collection of the sayings of Christ, said in old tradition to be the first form of his gospel, may have been already current in the Church. Mark's gospel was abroad, or about to be published. (2) Final salvation, and a further thrust against those who created the second problem in Timothy's diocese. "Keep the securities of the faith intact . . . guard most carefully your divine commission . . . turn a deaf ear to empty and worldly chatter, and the contradictions of what some miscall 'theology,' through which some, who have given their minds to it, have shot far wide of the faith" (20, 21 in various renderings). Do the "new theologians" ever read Paul?

Questions arising: (1) What is heresy? (2) Does doctrine matter? (3) What are the essentials?

You have heard Paul's answers. It is clear enough from this epistle that he believed that, by the quality of our living, and the clarity of our preaching we have a proclamation to make to this decade and this century. We must charge our spokesmen to deliver it, with authority and conviction. We must one and all demonstrate that there is one happy breed who can find zest for life, health of mind and creativity in self-control, chastity, and the age-old values of Christianity. Only thus shall we permeate society, and win a distracted mankind to Christ. There is a stinging word from Friedrich Nietzsche, he who provided the Nazis with some of their philosophy, and the Prussian theorists with their Blond Beast, and who invented the phrase: "God is dead." "You Christians," he said, "must look more redeemed, if you expect me to believe in your Redeemer." Even from such a source the challenge must be met.

QUESTIONS FOR DISCUSSION

(i) Consider the three questions raised at the close of the Introduction on page 62.

(ii) Consider the questions arising from verses 3 to 6 and listed at the end of the comments on that section on page 63.

(iii) List the qualities of the Christian "wise man."

(iv) In what sense is a Christian "self-sufficient"?

(v) The Christian and wealth in the New Testament.

(vi) Consider the three questions arising from verses 17 to 21 and listed on page 67.

Titus

INTRODUCTION

Within the narrow limits of the four or five years in which the Pastoral Epistles must fall, the letter to Titus must come near in time to the first letter to Timothy. Indeed, Paul could have written the two at the same time, perhaps during some week of comparatively free time when his mind turned to the need for organization in the churches he had founded.

A. *The Writer*

There is no need to doubt the Pauline authorship. This is the firmest of traditions, and tradition, as we have already observed, is not to be set aside save for the most compelling reasons. The chief reasons alleged against the authenticity of the epistle are (i) the language, and (ii) the situation in the church reflected in the text.

Take each in turn: (i) vocabulary and turn of phrase can form no basis of argument in such a brief text. Vocabulary depends upon subject matter, and style can be a matter of transient mood, time at the writer's disposal, the audience addressed, and many other matters. I myself, who write these notes with deliberate brevity, have this same week been busy on two tasks of popular journalism which have been mine for almost thirty years. I have written a Saturday editorial for a leading newspaper. This week it was on a theme of social medicine. I also wrote my customary contribution to a weekly paper, where, under a pen name, I discuss almost any subject. This week the theme was computers. Last week it was an archaeological discovery in Britain which recalled a poem of Housman. The vocabulary was quite different. So was the style. I have had the experience of writing the two articles at the same sitting and have actually felt a compulsion to change to another pen as I passed from the tightly written editorial to the more chatty and subjective column. Paul was seized with a sense of sudden urgency when he wrote to his two young ministers. He could see the looming of persecution, as Mark could when he wrote his gospel. Hence a laconic haste quite unmeasurable by computers or any other word-counting, and analyzing device. Of course, if Timothy or Titus edited the letters for general use, some vocabulary and stylistic phenomena would intrude. This would in no wise diminish authenticity or authority.

(ii) Paul had assessed events both in Rome and in Jerusalem. It was obvious that the whole weight of Rome would soon be brought to bear on rebellious Jewry. The Great Rebellion was in full view, and no one could speculate how deeply involved the Church would be in any disaster to international or metropolitan Jewry. No one could accurately foresee the special persecution which fell on the Church after the Great Fire of July 64, and the writing into law of anti-Christian legislation, but if the first letter to Timothy and the letter to Titus were written after that event, urgency was dire. The letters reflect exactly the situation in the sixties. The context of the next decade would not be nearly as appropriate.

It is naively assumed that the organization revealed in the pastoral epistles is the result of long evolution. Such an assumption calls for two comments. First, the directions laid down demonstrate that a system set up in the Church was not yet running automatically. Secondly, to set up a structure of the sort, in a world politically mature, could be a matter of weeks. Observe in the early chapters of Acts the rapidity with which the infant community organized its affairs.

B. *Historical Background*

Tentatively, we may assume the following timetable. Paul was released from his house-detention in Rome at some time after A.D. 62 but before the Neronian persecution in

64. He wrote the first letter to Timothy and the letter to Titus soon after release, probably before 64 but not necessarily before that date. It is difficult to trace his subsequent movements. It appears from First Timothy 1:3 that he had recently been at Ephesus, and had left that city for Macedonia. From Titus 1:5 it appears that he had visited Crete, where there seem to have been Christian groups. This and the visit to the Adriatic regions (Titus 3:12) were departures from the policy of planting churches in vital cities, which Paul had hitherto followed, though the change of strategic plan on a wider geographical pattern, does fit in with a possible visit to Spain at the same period (Rom. 15:24, 28). Crete, Dalmatia, Spain triangulate quite strikingly the central and western Mediterranean. In Second Timothy (1:16; 4:13; 4:20) place names are mentioned which suggest further journeys. In a word, scattered evidence suggests three or four years of characteristically vigorous activity in evangelism, or, more probably, in feverish organization in face of the growing threat. Paul may have been arrested in Troas in 66 or 67. He left his cloak and precious notes behind him, perhaps to avoid incriminating his hosts, or perhaps because he was roughly and hurriedly removed. He wrote the second letter to Timothy while in his last imprisonment, and died soon after, a martyr to his victorious faith.

[For further reading see the relevant articles in P.B.D. and N.B.D. and *The Century of the New Testament*.]

C. *The Recipient*

Titus, trusted companion of Paul, does not appear in the Acts. W. M. Ramsay has a theory that he was a relative of Luke, a suggestion which finds some support in Eusebius. On this theory, Luke omitted his name from the record in family modesty. Titus accompanied Paul and Barnabas to the Jerusalem conference, and, says Paul (Gal. 2:1, 3), was not compelled to conform to Jewish law. In all probability he was associated with some of Paul's journeys, but does not appear again until he fulfilled the office of special envoy to Corinth in a time of crisis in the church. He had served in some capacity in Corinth during the year preceding the writing of the second letter to the Corinthian church (2 Cor. 8:16-24). The unnamed Christian who accompanied Titus on this delicate mission is thought to be Luke, and if this is so some weight may be added to Ramsay's theory. It would appear from the second and seventh chapter of that epistle that Paul sent a letter of some severity to the Corinthians by Titus' hand, a document which has been lost. Titus then rejoined Paul in Macedonia (2 Cor. 7:6), bearing good news, which elicited the Second Epistle to the Corinthians. As far as we may piece these casual and incidental references together, it would seem that Titus was an ambassador in whom both Paul and the difficult church on the isthmus had confidence, and that a most difficult task of reconciliation was managed with tact and effectiveness (12:18).

Turning for further biographical hints to the letter addressed to him, it would appear that Titus accompanied Paul on his visit to Crete, and was left on the island to consolidate the church which was founded there (1:5, 6). The post was not permanent, for at the close of the letter (3:12), Paul speaks of replacing Titus by Artemas or Tychicus, and summons him to a rendezvous at Nicopolis, perhaps to conduct a mission in Dalmatia. He seems to have been in Dalmatia when Paul wrote his second letter to Timothy (4:10). Eusebius states that he returned to Crete and served there until old age.

It follows that Titus was a trusted and a valuable man, for Paul was not easily satisfied. He was a man for difficult assignments, strong, gracious, obviously sincere, and so trusted by all parties in a controversy. He was a good organizer and administrator. That is why he was in charge of the collection for the Jerusalem poor, that seemingly abortive project on which Paul set such store. He is a man seen, not in any full-length portrait, but by the movement of a hand, a passing shadow, as his presence, unobtrusive but strong, is felt, rather than seen, in trying and difficult situations. The Church can use such men.

I

CHAPTER ONE (1-16)

Introduction and Summary

The qualifications for office in the church here laid down should not be lightly disregarded. They are not irrelevant to the lay reader. KJV, with its reference to "bishops," has left those aspiring to less exalted office with the impression that the qualifications listed are irrelevant among the rank and file of the Christian society. In one New Testament sense all who own Christ's name are "priests" (Rev. 1:6; 5:10), and the chapter should be read by all Christians with the thought in mind that leadership in the Church is no prerogative of class or training but a high responsibility to which any member of Christ's community may at some time be called.

The chapter should be read over in various translations and pondered phrase by phrase. And let parents note with special care the challenging words of v. 6. A man can be disqualified by his family. It is true, as we have already said, that it is not always a parent's fault if children go astray, but it is a parent's first obligation to bend every effort to win his family first. What are the chief aids to this end? A parent should not be lofty and remote from his children, but friendly, humble, just, never refusing them time and fellowship, never too busy to talk, never posing or claiming perfection, ready to apologize, a loyal champion. Above all, never should two parents criticize or disparage another

Christian before children. Disillusionment comes early enough in life and in varied forms. There is no greater spiritual damage done to youth, than that which comes from disappointment with those who aspire to show the upward way, and are set up as examples of upright living.

A. *Verses 1 to 5*

1. Paul usually says "the slave of Jesus Christ" (Rom. 1:1; Phil. 1:1); "the slave of God, and the special messenger of Jesus Christ" is a variant of no significance. He was an apostle "for the confirmation of the faith of God's elect and for the spreading of the knowledge of the truth that goes with a godly life."

2. "Eternal life" is of wider significance than the life hereafter, as John's gospel, written thirty years later, was to stress. None the less, life indestructible is contained in the phrase, as Paul had emphasized, in language of some vigor, to the Corinthians (1 Cor. 15), and at this juncture of the world's history it was vital truth.

God's own truth, God's truthfulness, was involved in this deep faith.

3. God had revealed Himself in completeness and finality in Jesus Christ. It was done "in due time" by His living intrusion into history (John 1:1-18). It was historically the correct hour. The Greek word *kairos* implies this. The Roman Peace gave a framework for activity, and the Church took advantage of it for thirty years, before persecution began on the imperial plane. A second language, a basic Greek, was the common coinage of speech. At no other time had the stage of history been so set.

N.B. (i) Observe that it was "through preaching" that the message was made known. It can never be otherwise, though it is daunting to remember that most of those who at this date constituted the Church had few written documents in their hands. Mark was written about this time. Luke was at work on his books. Paul's letters were not collected and not widely circulated. The faith came to those who believed in an oral tradition, but on the lips of men of such undoubted sanctity and worth that it was believed, accepted, and passed on. We owe much to our first fathers in Christ.

(ii) The voices which decry preaching today, and propose to substitute something called "involvement," are the voices of those with no content left in their message to the world. We have a Gospel to preach, and we needs must preach it, in plain and relevant language. To preach Christ in the language of the day does not mean to demean or to diminish Him. The Bible can be related to the preoccupations of the decade without destroying its authority, without softening the impact of its uncompromising theism, without dethroning its Christ. The Church Militant must not surrender its sword. It must teach its men to use it.

4. What does the verse teach us of both Titus and Paul?

5. Literally: "I left you behind in Crete." Paul's visit to the long island, from which the Philistines had once come, seems certain. Christianity seems to have been in a disorganized state. Timothy, at Ephesus, seems to have been busy promoting and refining an existing structure of officers, presbyters (or elders) and deacons. Titus is bidden to set up elders as a basis for future elaboration. Crete needed, at this time, the fundamentals of an administration, in all centers of population. The "cities" of Crete were probably no larger than they are today, but Christian cells would appear to have been widespread.

B. *Verses 6 to 16*

6. See First Timothy 3:2 and 10. Look at the various renderings in the *Twenty-Six Translations* (Zondervan). It is a difficult matter in this critical world to be of irreproachable character, and unquestionable integrity. Such, however, should be the mark of anyone who leads the church. And dare any Christian opt for less?

We have dealt with the matters concerning marriage under the parallel verse in the first letter to Timothy, but note a firmer line about children in Crete. The direction either reflects a more rigorous family system in Crete, with parents held more firmly to blame for the conduct of their children, or else a more firmly established church in Ephesus. The submission of children to discipline is Paul's point.

7. A "steward of God" (Luke 12:42; 1 Cor. 9:17) must obviously be of unimpeachable uprightness, Paul repeats, not self-assertive (stubborn, arrogant, presumptuous, overbearing — are the various renderings), not bad-tempered, not a drinker, violent (see 1 Tim. 3:3 on these vices), not given to disreputable money-making ("no money-grabber," says NEB).

8. See First Timothy 3:2 on hospitality, and the same verse together with 2:9 on "soberness."

The last word implies self-control. Its roots are the noun for strength, and the preposition "in." It implies inner strength, the quality of which Paul spoke to Felix (KJV "temperance"). "Self-control," "mastery of passion" would suitably render the word.

["In the whole history of mankind, that power lacking the *inner strength* of *self-restraint* will eventually be cast down." *Adlai Stevenson.*

"Most powerful is he *who has himself in his own power.*" *Seneca.*

"No-one who cannot *master himself* is worthy to rule, and only he can rule." *Goethe.*]

9. Paul was insistent on holding fast to correct doctrine and, in consequence, refuting error. Conduct is linked to firm belief. It matters supremely what we believe, a fact that the present decade must learn anew. There was heresy abroad in Crete, some of it, no doubt, springing from Judaism, some from paganism.

10. This is clear from Paul's listing of dissidents and deviants, of whom the Jewish minority seem to have been the chief. The others were disorderly folk, "talkers with nothing to say" (Williams), of whom the church has always had a surfeit.

11. Such people should be muzzled. A sure method of dealing with a corrupting minority in a church is by all means to deny them opportunity to talk. Obviously they

must be denied office in teaching or administration. Allow such people to talk and they will inevitably deceive, and subvert. And their object is commonly "base gain" — and it would not be stretching the meaning to suggest that the gain can be measured in position, influence and standing as well as in cash.

12. The Cretans had a poor reputation in the ancient world. Paul quotes the poet Epimenides, himself a Cretan, whom he had quoted, in all probability, in his Areopagus address. Paul's line is a hexameter — *"The Cretans are liars all, wild beasts, just idolent bellies"* might render it.

13. They were, in fact, the fallen remnant of the great race which had established the pre-Greek Minoan civilization in the second millennium before Christ. Some vague folk-memory of a vanished might may have been a damaging psychological force in the Cretan proletariat. "Kretizein pros Kreta," to Cretize against a Cretan, was a proverb in Paul's time. It meant to lie to a liar. Epimenides was referring to the Cretan claim to hold in their island the tomb of Zeus—a curious form of thanatotheology, if such a word can be coined to touch the most outrageous heresy of recent times.

14. Titus, then, is to regard it a duty of leadership to stand firmly against the defects of the Cretan character, and especially against the machinations of the synagogues, the rabbis of which were at their old task of thrusting Judaism on the Church. See Mark 7:7, 8 and Colossians 2:22.

15. Paul's words are frequently misquoted and perverted. In origin the words may have been the Lord's own. Look at Mark 7:15-18 and Luke 11:41. See also Romans 14:20. The words must be set in the context of regulation-ridden Judaism, with its overwhelming list of "unclean" things. Gnosticism, the multiform perversion of Christianity which was emerging at the moment, had this in common with Judaism, that it was beginning to list a mass of taboos, to call the body, marriage and other natural practices of man, "unclean." Paul's point is that no one can in any way define sin, unless he begins with a life committed to God. To

evil men everything they touch, every human practice, joy, function, becomes evil. Horace, the Roman poet, had said a century before: "Unless the vessel be clean, whatever you put into it turns sour." A dirty mind soils all life. And the converse is true. If a man keeps his mind, as Isaiah put it, "stayed on God," his conscience and judgment are steadied and purified. If the "light that is in man, is itself darkness," as the Lord warned, no right decision in any moral question is possible.

16. These are the victims of the moral malady of the preceding verse. For all their blatant profession they do not know God.

QUESTIONS FOR DISCUSSION

(i) In the light of the fact that Paul made no abatement of his moral demands in establishing a church among the notorious Cretans, should any diminution of the moral and ethical requirements of Christianity be accepted or countenanced in any missionary context?

(ii) Is there in any sense a "new" morality?

(iii) "We must try to extend the frontiers of awareness into that transcendent dimension to which the present age has become so blind. That may be through study of the Bible, exposing ourselves to the impact of the gospels, as though we were now seeing them for the first time." Dr. F. R. Barry, former Bishop of Southwell, England. And what of the moral demands of the faith?

(iv) We have quoted above two Berkeley sociologists who have investigated the relation of belief to the practice of religion. They concluded "that a demythologized modernism is overwhelming the traditional Christ-centered faith," in some segments of the church, and that traditional belief lies beneath all other forms of commitment, attendance at church, the practice of prayer and Christian charity.

Discuss this in relation to the mingling of doctrine and conduct, faith and practice, in this chapter.

  (v) How quickly can a new church be organized?
 (vi) Is there need for fresh organization today?
(vii) How urgent are the times?
(viii) Disillusionment in youth.
 (ix) What is "eternal life"?
  (x) Can preaching get out of date?
 (xi) What Bible truths need stressing today?

II

CHAPTER TWO (1-15)

Introduction and Summary

There are chapters in the Bible so packed with exhortation and instruction that they should be frequently read. This chapter is one of them. Romans 12 and First Corinthians 13 are two others. At the same time it is to be admitted that words become a little worn with use. This chapter should therefore be read in one or two modern translations. It is a picture of Christian character in age and in youth. One Greek expression occurs as adjective, adverb and verb no fewer than five times in these fifteen verses. It is translated variously "temperate" (2), "teach to be sober" (4), "discreet" (5), "to be sober-minded" (6), "soberly" (12), and is a good illustration of the manner in which words change their meaning. "Sober" and "temperate" have lost their edge. The Greek word speaks of a wise self-control, as we have already seen, a strength of mind which knows how to avoid folly as well as vice, which shuns all excess, which keeps all desire, all activity, all thought, in rightful place. It suggests that it is a sane and ordered reason which makes for virtue, not mere emotion. The word sets the keynote for this crowded and challenging chapter. We shall turn to detail.

A. *Verses 1 to 10*

1. "But do you. . . ." Whatever the surrounding chaos and confusion, however ruinous the collapse of standards all around, whatever any heresy may bring to bear upon the

truth in persuasive error and blatant denial, do *you*, you the Christian, you the man whom Christ called to be different, do *you* stand firm in the sound conduct which befits sound belief? Look at First Timothy 6:11. Paul expected much of his young men — and found what he sought.

2. The chapter seems addressed to the laity at large. Some of the qualities enjoined have already been discussed in the notes on Timothy.

(a) Old men are graced by sobriety. It is significant to see this word, for which most of the translators favor "temperate," set at the head of the list. It has special relation to wine, and was so used in Classical Greek. It occurs at First Timothy 3:2, 11.

(b) . . . by gravity. The word was discussed at First Timothy 3:8. The quality is worth remembering in an age not noted for dignity, reserve, courtesy and polish in attitude and bearing.

(c) . . . by self-restraint. KJV uses "temperate" for this typically Greek quality. That word is best used under (a). "Over the years," says Barclay, who is particularly good in any discussion of Greek semantics, "the senior man must have acquired that cleansing, saving, strength of mind which has learned to govern every instinct and every passion, until each has its proper place, and no more than its proper place." Older men might note. The word was discussed in the parallel passage in the earlier epistle.

(d) The word under (c) suggests the rest of the verse which literally means: "showing health in faith, love, and steadfastness." This is exactly "sophron," the word so difficult to render. Unhealthiness can turn sound faith into credulity, love into sentimentality, steadfastness into obstinacy. A healthy faith trusts God with growing simplicity.

A healthy love grows wider in its tolerance, and deeper in its sympathy.

A healthy fortitude makes steadfastness less stressful, quieter, sweeter.

3. The older women had, as they always will have, a fine part to play. Their major marks in Christ are:

(a) "A reverent demeanor." This is a matter of bearing, speech, adornment, dress.

(b) "Not scandal-mongers" (1 Tim. 3:11; 2 Tim. 3:3).

(c) "Not slaves to drink." The Cretan women were notably "emancipated" in the island's early civilization. (It would be unfair to suggest that Delilah of a thousand years before [the Philistines were a colony from Crete] was in any way typical of the Cretan women of the mid-first century. Her breed is universal).

(d) "Teachers of virtue." Primarily by example.

4. The verse picks up the last word (d), and lists the prerequisites of a stable home. The Greek word for restrained, disciplined, balanced living occurs again.

5. The syllabus continues. Render: "sensible, chaste, good housewives, good women, in short, and loyal to their men, so that none shall sneer at the word of God." Christian homes are the best testimony a church can offer the community in which it labors.

6. The same self-discipline is urged upon the younger men ("sophron" again). See Proverbs 16:32. Self-mastery is a magnificent achievement for youth.

7. Titus was doubtless a member of the age-group thus addressed. He is called to a demanding task.

(a) As leader, he must be a model to the rest.

(b) . . . utterly sincere. Insincerity, posing of any sort, any lack of reality, gets through. There can be one motive only for preaching the Gospel — Christ's command.

(c) . . . dignified. See 2(b) above and First Timothy 3:8 where the same word occurs.

8. Continues the personal exhortation to Titus. A tremendous charge to the young minister.

9. and 10. The subject of slavery was discussed in the notes on the letter to Timothy. If these simple directions could be given to slaves, surely their spirit is applicable to the man who in freedom serves another in another world. There is a Christian attitude in employer and employee, and where any man is free to transfer his service, is not the obligation a lighter one than that which Paul enjoins on

those who had no such liberty? The world is rent with social and industrial discord, with harsh standing on one's rights, with swift-tongued self-defense. What a contribution to the wide-laid bases of man's peace could be made by a revival of Christian self-restraint, self-control, discretion. . . .

B. *Verses 11 to 15*

Barclay remarks (p. 293 of his book on the pastorals) that there are few passages in the New Testament which set forth "the moral power of the Incarnation" as vividly as this. The grace of God has appeared in Christ, God's offer to all men. Christ will come again. He redeemed us and set us apart.

But this is no empty privilege, no favor void of obligation. Interwoven with the theme of faith and saving conviction, indeed prominent in the whole passage, is the theme of conduct. The Christian is called to be different, apart, a new creation.

11. Donald Guthrie remarks (*Tyndale Commentary*, p. 198) that Paul cannot think of salvation apart from the grace of God (Eph. 2:8). This is characteristic Pauline thought, and one of those many marks of his authorship in the pastoral letters which far outweigh the alleged variations of language.

For "appeared" see First Timothy 6:14. The same verb is in Luke 1:79.

". . . to all men." Paul's great discovery of the global and universal Gospel never left the forefront of his teaching.

12. J. H. Bernard's comment, quoted by EGT at this place, is misleading. "The final cause of the revelation in Christ is not *creed* but *character*." There is a sense in which the words are true. Character, however, confirms creed. The two cannot be separated. There are those who impatiently abandon Christian belief, and stress the production of Christian character. This is not permanently possible. On the other hand (and this is the point James makes in his epistle), creed which produces no character consistent with it, is dead and useless.

Observe the three stages. The Christian, at his conversion, decides against carnal living, as being part of an accepted godless scheme rejected by him. He then begins a new life of self-control, goodness and trust in God.

"... a life of self-mastery, of integrity and of piety" (Moffatt).

"... responsible, honorable and God-fearing lives" (JBP).

"... lives of self-discipline, uprightness, and reverence towards God" (EMB).

"Worldly lusts" of KJV are the secular preoccupations of pagan society. The Vulgate says "desideria saecularia," the meaning of which is obvious. Compare Ephesians 2:3 and First Peter 4:2. "Stop trying to make yourselves like the society around you," says Romans 12:2, "but promote in your experience that new life which came to you, so that you may test out for yourselves the joy, the goodness and the perfection of the will of God."

13. The second Coming of Christ is a New Testament doctrine. It is a truth, indeed, a "blessed hope" which has been spoiled in clumsy hands, in schemes of date-fixing, and manifold folly. It has become the stock-in-trade of splinter sects which have bent and perverted a Christian truth in such destructive fashion that conservative Christians have hesitated wrongly to give it the place it should have in preaching and experience.

14. Three words should be stressed:

(a) "Redeem." Mark 10:45, First Timothy 2:6. A metaphor probably lifted from Psalm 129:8 where the Septuagint uses the whole phrase: "And He Himself, shall ransom Israel from all her acts of lawlessness."

(b) "Iniquity." "Lawlessness" is the exact word. The rejection of God's standards, with their demands upon life, defiance of eternal law, lie at the foundation of all sin. Sin, from Adam on, is rebellion.

(c) "Peculiar." The sense is: "purify and so make them fit to be his people." Paul has in mind, consciously or unconsciously, Ezekiel 37:23. (Perhaps this also reveals his knowledge of the incident which John was to relate in his third chapter. There Christ speaks to Nicodemus in the imagery of Ezekiel 36 and 37. Paul, like Nicodemus, probably had the Old Testament by heart.)

The word "peculiar" comes from Exodus 19:5.

". . . a people for his own possession" (ASV)

". . . a people to be His very own" (Williams)

". . . a pure people marked out for His own" (NEB)

Had Paul also Malachi 3:17 in mind?

15. This is the Christian preacher's message. It should be delivered with authority and confidence. How very relevant is this timeless direction today.

The primary question before the church today is not how to organize its institutions, but whether Christianity is true; and if its spokesmen appear to be uncertain, what hope is there for the layman? . . . If the church gives the impression of regarding the Gospel itself as an open question, and the being of God as no more than an interesting hypothesis, has it anything important left to say?

We have a Gospel to preach, and we needs must preach it, in plain and relevant language. To preach Christ in the language of the day must not diminish Him. To relate the Bible to the contemporary scene must not weaken its authority. A salutary social awareness must not blind us to the fact that Christianity begins with a personal and individual commitment to Christ, and that all preaching, for all its wider awareness, must address itself to each man and woman.

QUESTIONS FOR DISCUSSION

    (i) The status of women in the church and society. What is the Christian attitude? Is Paul still relevant?

   (ii) The Christian workman, his loyalties and his obligations.

  (iii) Dignity in worship.

  (iv) Dogmatism in the pulpit.

   (v) Authority in witness.

  (vi) Can we modify any of Paul's requirements today?

 (vii) Define sincerity. Can insincerity be hidden?

C. *Reading*

William Barclay's two books, *A New Testament Word-book* and *More New Testament Words*, contain material of absorbing interest. He is an extremely sound Greek scholar, and approaches New Testament Greek, as it should be approached, from the angle of Classical Greek. In the first listed book, he has a chapter on "Lutron" — a "ransom" (p. 76), and in the second a chapter on "semnos" — "grave" (p. 140).

III

CHAPTER THREE (1-15)

Introduction and Summary

The picture of the Christian continues, but with emphasis now on his place in society. Paul's preaching, for all its lofty flights, had its feet set firmly upon the ground. He knew how much depended upon the Christian's conduct in society. Consider the plain common sense of the opening words of this chapter as Phillips renders them: "Remind your people to recognize the power of those who rule and bear authority. They must obey the laws of the state and be prepared to render whatever good service they can. They are not to speak evil of any man, they must not be argumentative but gentle, showing themselves to be agreeable to everybody. . . ." Paul intends his words to be read with proper reservations. A command to do evil should not be obeyed, and lofty tribunals in our own day have established that principle against criminals who have alleged military orders for excuse. Nor does the duty to be agreeable involve compromise. Courtesy, helpfulness, readiness to serve and do one's duty, scrupulous honesty, friendliness — these and their simple like are fruits of the Spirit. They are also an essential part of a Christian testimony, and there are those who lose the way to Christ for the lack of such graces in professing Christians. A Christian testimony comprises doing as well as saying; participating as well as abstaining; involvement as well as withdrawal; the secular as well as the sacred; weekdays as well as Sundays; our daily work as well as our religious activities . . . all in right proportion and place. A Christian never ceases to be a Christian and to be regarded as one.

A. *Verses 1 and 2*

Paul's visit to Crete seems to have confirmed in his mind the poor reputation in which the islanders were held in the ancient world. The occupying Nazis in the Second World War found the population impossible to subdue. A passionate independence, with by-products of lawlessness, is often the mark of the population of rugged islands. Witness the history of Corsica and Sardinia through the centuries.

Hence, an intractable trait in the Cretan character, and Paul's anxiety that church communities should submit to properly constituted authority. Compare Romans 13 and First Peter 2:13ff for Paul's careful directions about the Christian and government. In First Timothy 2:1-3 Christians of Asia are bidden to pray for their rulers. In Titus the more simple duty of obedience is stressed. Paul deprecates defamation and brawling, and commends gentleness and meekness, qualities not likely to come easily to the typical Cretan. Meekness contains courtesy, that last fine fruit of culture. And who should be more cultured than the Christian?

B. *Verses 3 to 7*

Lest the Cretans should feel resentful, Paul speaks of the past. It was the love of God, he says, which saved many who professed Christ from folly, disobedience, self-deception, enslavement to carnality, lives of evil and envy and mutual hate (4).

Such salvation was all due to the goodness and grace of God (5), an attitude not springing from works of righteousness done by us, but because He was merciful, and brought us to new life and renewing through His Spirit which he generously gave (6).

(Consider how completely Pauline is this thought.)

In v. 7 the great evangelical passage rounds off. Perhaps it was a form of words sung as a hymn. The theory of ordered hymns embedded in the text of Pauline epistles is probably a sound one. The oral tradition tended to fall into set forms. Look up the passages which begin: "I received of the Lord . . ." It requires some effort of the imagination to grasp the position of doctrine in a church without the New Testament.

C. *Verses 8 to 11*

Hence, the need for firm and constant emphasis (8). Belief in God and in Christ, Paul insists, is not a matter of theory, formula, or speculation, but of character and good works. But observe, too, how vulnerable, in the absence of an authoritative New Testament, the church may have been to deviant and heretical doctrine, and the need to deal firmly with such dissidents.

"Heresy" is the Greek *hairesis* which simply means "a choice." Hence its non-offensive use for "sect" in Acts 5:17; 15:5; 26:5. The Jews also called the Christians a *hairesis* in Acts 24:5 and 28:22, and here the word begins to assume its pejorative color. In 24:14 Paul appears to object to the tone of the word, and in KJV the translation reflects his objection, though most other translations maintain consistency with the earlier verse (5), and render accordingly. Paul himself uses the word pejoratively in First Corinthians 11:19 and Galatians 5:20. So does Peter (2.2:1). It follows that in the present context the best translations are "factious man" (ASV), "sectarian" (Con.) or "a man who causes divisions" (TCNT). Or, better, "a wilful dissident."

A specific case may be in mind — "recognizing that such a person has a bent mind and is self-condemned in his wrongdoing." Self-condemned, presumably by his own separation, like those castigated by John (1.2:19).

D. *Verses 12 to 15*

Artemas, probably short for Artemidoros, as Epaphras was for Epaphraditos, is otherwise unknown. Tychicus was a trusted messenger (Col. 4:7; Eph. 6:21). Nicopolis was in Dalmatia, the ancient Epirus. It was a foundation of Augustus and a school of the Stoic Epictetus was located there in the nineties of the century. In 31 B.C. the Battle of

Actium was fought nearby — one of the decisive battles of the world. It insured the continued unity of the Empire, and the concentration of power in the hands of Octavian, who was to be the Emperor Augustus.

Artemas and Tychicus were to take over from Titus. Apollos is known from Acts (18:24). See P.B.D. Zenas was a converted rabbi (a "lawyer"). This is the more probable explanation. It is just possible that Zenas was a Greek secular lawyer. Both these men appear to have been in Crete, or to be passing that way before Titus' projected departure.

The letter ends with the formal salutations which concluded ancient letters. See Chapter 8: "Archaeology and the Epistles," from *Archaeology of the New Testament* (Zondervan) by E. M. Blaiklock.

QUESTIONS FOR DISCUSSION

(i)   The Christian and the law of the land.
(ii) Conscientious objection and dissent.
(iii) The Church and heresy.
(iv) Tolerance of dissent.
(v)   The place of compromise on moral issues.
(vi) Is the Christian accepted in worldly society without compromise on his part? Is an honorable popularity possible? Will a true Christian ever be without enemies?
(vii) Reconstruct some of the "oral tradition" of the first century Church.
(viii) Is it more difficult for some people to form disciplined Christian communities than for others? Consider various mission fields. Is there a need for tolerance, understanding or special teaching here?

2 Timothy

INTRODUCTION

We have dealt with the matters of writer and recipient. This letter is Paul's last utterance. Paul was arrested, perhaps around the years 66 or 67, and probably at Troas, under the anti-Christian legislation which was promulgated in Rome after Nero's panic-stricken persecution of the Christians which began in 64. As a Roman citizen, he was sent to Rome for trial. The end would have appeared inevitable. The last chapter at least, probably the whole epistle, was written from prison.

This letter is a moving document, more personal in tone than the two other pastoral letters, and preoccupied with Timothy himself, a theme which occupies a third of the letter. A second long section (2:14-4:5) treats of the future of the church in the dark days which were looming. Finally, the great man speaks of himself. It would require a considerable master of literature to compile a fiction so convincing. It is difficult to see how any informed and sensitive reader could deny the epistle its traditional authenticity.

As Alfred Plummer wrote in the Expositor's Bible (5.461) almost a century ago: "We have Paul with his exquisite sympathy, sensitiveness and affection, his intense anxiety, his unflinching courage. We have the sincerity and importunity of one who knows his days are numbered. And we have the urgency and tenderness of one who writes to a friend who has his faults and weaknesses, but who is trusted and loved spite of them."

[Plummer's leisurely Victorian commentary on the Pastoral Epistles in EB is, in fact, very well worth quiet study.]

I

CHAPTER ONE (1-18)

Introduction and Summary

After a formal opening, as common as "Dear Timothy" would be today, Paul seeks to hand on the torch. Timothy was in Ephesus — one young man at the head of a small devoted band at grips with the organized and commercialized (Acts 19) paganism of a great city. Paul sets out to strengthen and encourage the young leader. He tells him of his prayers and confidence in him. He reminds him of the noble tradition of his family and of the call of God. Such exhortation and encouragement are a ministry which older men should covet and exercise. To be aloof, unapproachable, gruff, and impatient with youth, is not part of the Spirit of Christ. Scorn and sarcasm are of the devil. Youth is the inevitable successor. The years themselves insure that one day other hands will hold the helm, and other minds will plan. To train those hands, and inspire those minds, should be the task of present leadership. To embitter and frustrate them is no service to the cause of Christ which it will be their task to promote. Paul seeks to pass on his own unshaken confidence, and his uncorrupted message.

A. *Verses 1 and 2*

Perhaps the formality of the opening salutation, with Paul's official title, indicates that part at least of the letter was destined for a wider public than Timothy, the immediate recipient. The realization may have been taking shape in Paul's mind that an authoritative corpus of documents was taking shape. Peter had already envisaged that necessity, and set Mark to work on his gospel (2 Pet. 1:15, 16). Luke's gospel, and probably Acts, was, along with Mark's brief account, in the hands of the church. Matthew's collection of the sayings of Christ had probably not yet been rounded into the first gospel. The majority of the epistles were circulating.

"The preciousness of the promise," says N. J. D. White in EGT, on v. 1, "is never wholly absent from the minds of Christians; though of course it comes to the surface of our consciousness at crises when death is, or seems to be imminent." It is against the most fundamental instincts of man's nature to suppose that anything resembling religion can survive the passing of the hope of another life.

Consider two quotations from Tennyson:

> *Thou wilt not leave us in the dust,*
> *Thou madest man, he knows not why;*
> *He thinks he was not made to die;*
> *And thou hast made him: thou art just.*
>   *In Memoriam.*
>
> *Truth for Truth and Good for Good! The Good, the True,*
>   *the Pure, the Just —*
> *Take the charm "For ever" from them, and they crumble*
>   *into dust.*
>   *Sixty Years After.*

B. *Verses 3 to 7*

It may be demonstrated from the epistle to the Philippians (see *From Prison in Rome* by E. M. Blaiklock, Pickering & Inglis) that Paul was the most tactful of men. He intends a gentle rebuke against what he considers a certain lack of moral courage in Timothy. It appears in v. 7. Verses 3 to 6 are full of commendation. So in the Philippians letter. A rebuke to two women appears, but not till Chapter Three, when the community has been praised, exhorted to unity, thanked for loyalty and goodwill.

Some details:

3. Paul had served God "from his forefathers." See Acts 22:3 and 24:14; Romans 11:1; Second Corinthians 11:22; Philippians 3:5. Then Acts 26:6. This will give the drift of

his thought. It is consonant with his steady contention that
Christianity was not a new religion, but the logical and
divinely purposed sequel and fulfillment of Judaism. He had
simply moved on with God's plan. In this stance he was
quietly confident. See Second Corinthians 1:12.

4. A keen memory was Timothy's grief at their last
parting, and that recollection was forthwith transmuted into
a Godward desire. Tears, in the ancient world, were a less
inhibited expression of emotion than they are today — at
least among self-repressed Anglo-Saxons.

5. An heir of faith for two loyal generations, a man
genuinely convinced, and further strengthened by the confidence born of a (6) formal ordination, should, in similar
mindfulness to Paul's own, be conscious of his gifts, nourish
and promote their exercise, and — (7) now comes the point,
not be timid, diffident or backward.

To rule the church at Ephesus Timothy needed:
- (a) strength of character, a quality which, perhaps
  oversheltered by a widowed (?) mother and grand-
  mother, the young man needed to lay hold of and
  develop;
- (b) love, not soft indulgence but pity and compassion
  which nevertheless tolerated no intruding sin;
- (c) self-discipline (*sophronismos*) which, in strong
  and balanced sanity steadied self and others.

C. *Verses 8 to 14*

8. There is no need to suppose that Timothy had found
his association with Paul a social stigma, but there was such
a temptation looming.

People of natural or constitutional timidity are sensitive
to the sneers or ridicule of others, however cheap or con-
temptible they are.

(a) In the academic environment a Christian is sometimes made to feel that his acceptance of Christian belief
is a mark against his standards of objective scholarship,

where the cult of the suspended judgment holds sway. The Christian must be prepared for this as part of what he owes to Christ, and proceed, in matters of professional scholarship and devotion to his discipline or teaching, to demonstrate his excellence.

(b) In the business world the Christian is sometimes derided for a sensitive conscience which denies him opportunities for making money and securing personal advantage. Here, as elsewhere, there is what C. S. Lewis, in an essay under that title, called "the inner ring." When in scrupulous exercise of conscience, the Christian refuses to take the step which secures acceptance, he is branded a timid fool.

(c) Among young people the Christian who holds to chastity, honor, self-control, abstinence or other marks of disciplined living in the name of Christ, is sometimes made to feel a coward. It is the coward who weakly conforms.

There are times in their contest for the faith when the faithful feel lonely. The remnant is a theme in the Old Testament. It is a thread through all history. But these can sense the chill of loneliness. "I, even I only, am left, and they seek my life to destroy it" . . . or read Psalm 3, that prayer of the old guerrilla fighter as dawn paled over Moab, and he backed with a remnant from the fallen city and his rebel son to the familiar refuge of the wilderness. "Many, many, many . . ." runs through the prayer like a dull refrain. A word thirty years old comes from the Cabinet Room in Downing Street. France was down, and Churchill, back from Bordeaux, reported his failure to persuade the crumpled ally to stand. "And so, gentlemen," he said, "we stand alone." There was silence, and tense faces round the long table. The old bulldog looked round, and slowly said: "I find it rather exhilarating."

This is what Paul feared for a man naturally not brave. By exhortation and personal example he sought to nerve him for the challenge to come.

9 and 10 are perhaps a formal hymn in which the Church embedded and preserved its fundamental belief. It

is on the basis of our standing in Christ, the call of God, His grace bestowed, the eternal plan of which we form a part, of our hope of life more abundant, that, whatever comes, we should not fear, but stand unyielding.

11 and 12 stress Paul's personal example. Verse 12 is one of the finest testimonies in Scripture. Faith grows into knowledge. Steadfastness in belief produces the vast evidence of experience. Continuing in faith, unafraid, undaunted, brings that which approaches certainty. Doubt, to be sure, can attack any Christian, but doubt is not a way of life. It should be answered by prayer and renewed committal.

"That which I have entrusted to Him" — "my deposit" (Ber.); "the treasure I have committed to Him" (Con.). The metaphor is the practice of entrusting something precious to another for safekeeping on solemn oath. Our persons are precious. Christ died for them. He is the perfect guardian and will hold until we are complete.

It follows that in daily practice a Christian may commit to his Lord his:

career		vindication
reputation		fulfillment
marriage		honor
business	against the day of	satisfaction
profession		judgment
integrity		— or whatever
— what you will		applies

13. "A form of sound words." Our language in Christian testimony should be well-chosen, clear, persuasive, true to Scripture and (14) revelation, worthy of the precious Gospel left in our feeble hands, and of the indwelling God who hears every word, and penetrates each thought.

D. *Verses 15 to 18*

Paul was not the only example of courage and loyalty. Many had turned away from their old teacher in Timothy's own province. Perhaps there is point here for Timothy who is thus warned against current tongues of disloyalty, like those of Phygellas and Hermogenes, both so unlike the late Onesiphorus, who, clearly dead now, had stood by the prisoner of Christ with all its attendant risks, as he had done beforetime in Ephesus, his home-city. "He sought me out," says Paul, and the picture emerges of the man from Asia in the teeming metropolis of a million souls, pressing his inquiries until he discovered the whereabouts of the doomed and imprisoned man. There is worth and beauty in loyal friendship. Onesiphorus, however he may have subsequently died, merits our memory and regard.

QUESTIONS FOR DISCUSSION

(i) Conscience is the root for all true courage. If a man would be brave let him obey his conscience.

(ii) "Courage consists not in hazarding without fear, but being resolutely minded in a good cause" (Plutarch).

(iii) "Trust men and they will be true to you" (Emerson).

(iv) "Confidence in another man's virtue is no slight evidence of one's own" (Montaigne).

(v) The need for a written record, and the importance today of an authoritative Bible. Can the Church exist with less than this?

(vi) How vital in Christian belief is confidence in an after-life? On what is such faith based?

(vii) The loneliness of the Christian. What is popularity worth?

(viii) What have we trusted to Christ for Him to keep? Against what day?

(ix) "Moral courage is the rarest of virtues." Is it? If so, why?

II

CHAPTER TWO (1-26)

Introduction and Summary

An obligation lies upon the Christian to transmit and
propagate his faith. Timothy is bidden to commit the Gospel
to faithful men. Thus have we received it; and on each one
who thus receives Christ lies the responsibility of giving the
truth to others. It is a task for faithful men, men who can be
trusted to tell the whole truth, men who can be relied upon
in times of stress to remain loyal to Christ, men who so
watch and guard their manner of living that Christ may
suffer no diminution in the eyes of the watching world.
All Christians are in some sense preachers of the Gospel,
and fall under the obligation to be faithful in this way. A
light is not for hiding under a bushel, but for the con-
venience of all in the house. The Christian parent must seek
by all means to pass on his faith to his children. It is the
foremost duty which lies on him, of greater moment than
all other tasks of witness. The Christian must exercise the
discipline of the soldier, the patience of the husbandman,
the dedication of the athlete — remembering always that he
is not alone, but that Christ, raised from the dead, stands
with him. Certain now that his own time was short, Paul
bends every effort to the task of moulding Timothy into a
strong Christian leader. From his eloquent words a challenging picture takes shape. The useful Christian is clean and
upright in character, patient, gentle with the ignorant, and
those who are slow of understanding. His continual desire
is so to work that his Master will commend his craftsman-

ship; he is ambitious to be used for the loftiest and noblest ends. He holds his faith firmly and simply, seeking always to set it before men positively and plainly. He avoids speculation, unfruitful discussion, and vain controversy. This warning is repeated twice (14, 16). Paul by no means implies that there are not occasions when a firm stand must be taken on an issue of truth or sound doctrine. His own letters, even the pastorals, are evidence that he did not fear and deplore those intrusions of intellectual arrogance which have, in all ages, produced damaging heresies. Difficulties and questions must be faced, and it is a teacher's duty to answer with patience and clarity. He does deplore (and how timelessly relevant are his words) perverse search for novel interpretations, the raising of doubt for argument's sake, and unprofitable debate.

A. *Verses 1 to 10*

1. "Be strong." Look at the first chapter of Joshua where, in like fashion, a veteran hands over to a younger man. The verse resumes the thread broken after 1:8, 9. The verb, which implies inner strength, is found also at First Timothy 1:12; Romans 4:20; Ephesians 6:10; Philippians 4:13. The verb, it should be pointed out, is in one of those forms shared by the Middle and Passive Voices. In other words, it means both "be strengthened" and "strengthen yourself." There is no need to choose which voice was prominent. It is sound theology to see both in salutary partnership. Grace and faith must mingle to avail. "Abide in me and I in you." (We might pause at this point to suggest again to serious students of the New Testament, that the acquisition of even a little Greek opens wide vistas of understanding. It is not a difficult language.)

The word "grace" has its simple meaning of the help which comes from God.

2. Here is the apostolic succession indeed. Christianity depended upon historic fact. Here is a teacher of the first century, a man of great intellectual power, directing that the faith be transmitted intact, with the historical detail on

which it depended, passed on accurately and fully to men prepared faithfully in their turn to pass it to yet another generation. How far is this situation from that imagined by some forms of modern literary criticism which pictures a Church, come into being one knows not how, and inventing progressively a historical background for inexplicable forms of worship and organization with which it somehow found itself provided.

3. The next three verses illustrate the patent fact that the task involves battle (3 and 4), dedication (5), toil (6). See Philippians 2:25; Philemon 2. (The same three word-pictures are similarly juxtaposed at 1 Cor. 9:6, 6-10, 24-27.)

4. Paul was well acquainted with Stoic thought. After all, two of the founders of Stoicism came from Cilicia. A study of Paul's words often reveals echoes of Stoic sayings. The Areopagus Address, and the first four chapters of the first letter to Corinth, are full of illustration. It is also interesting that Seneca, who was more of a Stoic than anything else, and Epictetus, who founded a Stoic school, should both use the metaphor of soldiering with its overriding demands on the conduct of life. "To live," said the first-named, "is to be a soldier" (*Ep. Mor.* 95.6). And Epictetus: "The life of every man is a kind of campaign, long and varied." The metaphor embodies obedience, loyalty, self-sacrifice.

5. Competitors in the Greek games were required to state on oath that they had undergone training. In other words, they were disciplined men. In the contest they were required to observe the rules. The ministry of the Church requires the same dedication, the same will to win, the same respect for authority (Heb. 12:1).

6. "The hard-working farmer" (RSV) provides the third illustration of Christian toil. He must be prepared to sow and have another reap, to battle with weeds and pests, to discover unfruitful soil, and crops which disappoint. (Read Masefield's poem *The Everlasting Mercy,* especially the musings of Saul Kane, the morning after his conversion, as he leans over the farm-gate and watches the plowman.)

7. Stop, now, says Paul, and consider what I say. He refers to his three word-pictures. Obey him. Pause here, and with a concordance follow his three metaphors through. *The Zondervan Topical Bible* will provide many relevant headings.

8. Christ Himself was the supreme example of soldier, athlete, farmer. Note again that, in Paul's mind a gospel was no gospel without the central truth of the Resurrection. The verb is in the present imperative: "keep on remembering"; "bear steadfastly in mind."

9. The imprisoned Christian was called "a malefactor." In Chapter 11 of his *Church in the Roman Empire*, W. M. Ramsay writes of Nero's persecution, and shows that this very term was characteristic of the Neronian period (p. 249).

10. See Philippians 1:12, 14 and 6:17 below. Paul does not suggest that he could preach as he had been able to do during his earlier detention in Rome. He owed it to "the elect" to stand firm.

B. *Verses 11 to 13*

Paul could write rhythmic prose. Sir William Ramsay, whom we quoted in another context under v. 9, demonstrated that fact in a notable essay (*The Teaching of Saint Paul in Terms of the Present Day*, pp. 412 ff). At the same time the theory that there is a good deal of quotation from a primitive Christian hymnology in his letters, has a certain plausibility. The hymn is a good vehicle of Scriptural truth — a fact to be steadfastly borne in mind by those who write or choose hymns. If the theory be true, these three verses would qualify as a good example. For the metaphor of dying and rising with Christ see Romans 6.

C. *Verses 14 to 26*

14. "These things" are the issues set forth in the hymn. "Keep on reminding them of these truths, urging them with all solemnity, as in the sight of God, to abjure wrangling about words, which helps no one, but unsettles those who hear."

The Greeks loved words and philosophic disputation. They were not the only ones with this unprofitable fault. The remedy is plain, simple preaching with the note of Scriptural authority. God knows, in the lamentable theological confusion of today, with the double-talk of philosophical theology invading the pulpit, the advice is timely and relevant.

Read this section through in several translations.

15. "Try hard to show yourself worthy of God's approval (NEB), a workman who does not need to be ashamed of his work (Knox), driving a straight furrow in the proclamation of the truth" (NEB).

It is difficult to be sure of the final metaphor. NEB takes it as the plowman's straight line; "Following a straight course in the preaching of the truth," says the more recent NAB; "who drives the plowshare of truth in a straight furrow," says A. S. Way's little-known translation. Perhaps NEB and Way are correct, and Paul still has his farming metaphor in mind.

16. ". . . godless, idle chatter," once tolerated "goes from bad to worse," is Paul's downright opinion.

It is good policy to deny the purveyors of heresy in any congregation the opportunity to talk. They should be excluded from teaching or preaching, because they are often exhibitionist, arrogant and talkative types who thrive on wordiness. Such is Paul's advice. It is no assault on freedom of speech. It is protection for freedom of hearing.

17. Allow heresy and folly free play, and it spreads like a gangrene (the actual Greek word). Paul may have learned the medical term from Luke.

18. Two of the pests in the Ephesian church have been named. Their particular heresy seems to have centered in the Resurrection. We can only guess what lay behind their particular perversion.

(a) Perhaps they were Jews infected with the Sadducean denial of life beyond the grave (see *Sadducee* in a Bible Dictionary).

(b) Perhaps they were tinged with Stoic doctrine. The

Stoics thought of the soul as a spark from God, absorbed at death into that from which it came, or extinguished.

(c) Not unlike those today who make a metaphor out of the Resurrection, some were asserting that the doctrine spoke only of "rising with Christ" at baptism (Rom. 6).

[It might be well to pause at this point and stress the essentials of the doctrine.

1. Speaking of a similarly dissident group at Corinth, Paul, in the most emphatic terms, set the Resurrection down as a basic and essential doctrine of the faith (1 Cor. 15).

2. He meant the historical rising of Christ from the dead — the Christian explanation, based on visual evidence, of the attested fact of the empty tomb.

3. The gospels present the evidence in authenticated detail. It is possible only to look upon the relevant chapters as history. They admit of no allegorical or metaphorical interpretation. They must stand or fall as serious narrative of observed fact.]

19. Paul was fond of the metaphor of a foundation. It crept into his vocabulary after his visit to Athens, where he saw the Parthenon, mightily founded on the rock of the Acropolis (See 1 Tim. 3:15; 1 Cor. 3:10-15; Eph. 2:19-23).

Perhaps the metaphor of the seal is another word-picture, with Paul guilty of a "mixed metaphor." Moffatt and Knox, however, think of the word as an inscription. The oracular shrine of Delphi, the temple of Apollo, had an inscription at either end. On the front was: "Know thyself"; on the other end: "Nothing in excess." Perhaps Paul thought of something like this, saw in swift thought the foundation crowned with the temple of God, and set the two warning inscriptions upon it.

20, 21. These verses are to be taken together and are a little difficult to interpret, perhaps because of an over-compactness of thought.

The picture Paul has in mind is a great house. The thought has crossed his mind: "Why are such people as Hymenaeus and Philetas allowed in the Church at all?" The Parable of the Wheat and the Tares (Matt. 13:24-30, 36-43), and the Parable of the Drag-Net (Matt. 13:47, 48), had touched on this problem — the mingling of all sorts and conditions in the visible church, the inevitable task of separation, and ultimate purification.

He pictures a house with all sorts of vessels, some of gold and silver, jealously kept, some of crude Samian ware, cast out with little thought. The master alone can determine ultimate value. The analogy breaks down, as all analogies somewhere do, at the point of personal choice. A man can be the vessel he desires to be, cleansed and "fit for the master's use."

22. The thought suggests a warning to Timothy. (See the chapter on Ephesus in *Cities of the New Testament*, by E. M. Blaiklock, Pickering & Inglis.) Carnality was rife in the Asian city. It centered in the worship of Artemis with its "sacred prostitution." A young man was not above temptation. Hence a paternal warning. Timothy has been warned against the sins of the intellect. Paul thinks it proper to warn him against the temptations of the flesh and to commend those qualities which grow out of a heart committed to Christ.

23. With which, as though it was heavily upon his mind, Paul reverts to the ignorant and wordy controversies he has already deprecated. In his didactic method, as he told the Philippians, he never shunned repetition (Phil. 3:1, 18).

24. "Gentle to all men, so that he will be apt to teach; forbearing towards opponents, so that he will be able to correct" (Bengel).

25 and 26 close the chapter with the thought, arising from the last word of 24, that the nuisances and the trouble-makers in the church were not beyond redemption. The yearning of the apostle's mind and heart over those whose

error he had so vigorously castigated emerges as he closes this section of the letter. The "vessels of dishonor" were something more than clay. They were salvageable.

QUESTIONS FOR DISCUSSION

(i) "Meekness excludes revenge, irritability and morbid sensitiveness, but not self-defense, or a quiet and steady maintenance of right" (Bishop Theophylact of Byzantium, 11th century).

(ii) "All the noises and prating of the pool, the croaking of frogs and toads, are hushed by the bringing upon them of a candle or a torch."   (Jeremy Taylor)

(iii) "If Christ be not risen from the dead we are of all men the most miserable" (Paul). The historical reality of the Resurrection. Consider the doctrine in relation to Paul's position.

(iv) "What Cicero said of war, may be applied to controversy — it should always be so managed as to remember that the only true end of it is peace" (Pope). When is controversy necessary?

(v) The useful and the useless Christian.

(vi) Soldiering for Christ. Consider the word-picture.

III

CHAPTER THREE (1-17)

Introduction and Summary

The chapter opens with a shocking picture of a godless society. It is not by accident that it so fits the modern scene in this increasingly urbanized world. Of all the centuries, this latter half of the twentieth is most like the latter half of the first, city-ridden, marred by manifold tyrrany, decadent, and wracked by financial and even ecological crisis.

Where Christ holds no sway thought fast becomes "a crawling ruin," and life "a leaping mire," as Chesterton put it in the magnificent poem we have already quoted, *The Ballad of the White Horse.* In the midst of such abounding sin stands the spiritual evil of formal religion, that patronage of God and lip-service to traditional forms which is too often found in sections of society which veneer godlessness with respectability, and find a back-slidden Church ready to compromise. Then, too, is found the nefarious activity of others who seek profit in corrupt religion and find their victims among the foolish, the emotional, and the unbalanced. It is, in fact, assuming contemporary significance. To sharpen this point, read the first five verses in Taylor's free translation: "You may as well know this too, Timothy, that in the last days it is going to be very difficult to be a Christian. For people will love only themselves and their money; they will be proud and boastful, sneering at God, disobedient to their parents, ungrateful to them and bad. They will be hard-hearted, and never give in to others; they will be constant liars and troublemakers, and will think nothing of immorality . . . hot-headed, puffed up with pride, and prefer good times to worshipping God. They will go to church, yes, but they won't believe anything that they hear." (*Living Letters*) Paul's prophecy is astonishingly accurate.

In such a society the Christian who stands firm and preaches the truth can expect persecution. It is an inevitable reaction of those committed to godless living to resent the challenge of a godly testimony. The response, in the seventies of the twentieth century, as in the sixties of the first, must be steadfastness fed by the knowledge that evil will pass away, by the assurance which experience brings, by the Scriptures and their comfort, and by the memory of godly example.

A. *Verses 1 to 9*

1. It is idle to speculate whether Paul thought that "the last times" and, by implication, Christ's second intrusion into human history, were upon them. It was his duty then, as it is ours now, so to live, so to preach, so to wait, as if any moment might see history's consummation. The times were dire and difficult enough. There are Christians at this moment, who should constantly be in our prayers, who cannot but think, and indeed fervently hope, that the end of the age with its "Great Tribulation" is at hand.

(See 2 Pet. 3; Jude 18; 1 John 2:18; 1 Tim. 4:1.)

"Difficult, troublesome, or dangerous times" are not confined by time or place. This much can be said, that today, as never before in this century, responsible voices, laymen along with churchmen, are loud in warning of some day of dire reckoning. The world needs desperately a vast religious revival. It is no time for heretical posturing, for compromise, for trifling in the pulpit, for fumbling the task of the church. There is no place left save for those in whose heart Christ's Gospel burns.

2-5. For the list of vices cursing Nero's world see Romans 1:29 ff. We shall not analyze each noisome term. The *Twenty-Six Translations* provides facets enough of somber meaning, and each facet reflects this morning's news.

But note one or two points: (a) despisers of the good. It is a mark of evil's ultimate degradation to hate the good. Nero's persecution was still falling on the Christian community of Rome when Paul was writing. Telling the story of the Fire of Rome, forty years later, Tacitus wrote:

> But neither human aid, nor imperial bounty, nor atoning-offerings to the gods, could remove the sinister suspicion that the fire had been brought about by Nero's order. To put an end therefore to this rumour, he shifted the charge on to others, and inflicted the most cruel tortures upon a body of men detested for their abominations, and popularly known by the name of Christians. This name came from one Christus, who was put to death in the reign of Tiberius by the Procurator Pontius Pilate; but though checked for the time, the detestable superstition broke out again, not in Judaea only, where the mischief began, but even in Rome, where every horrible and shameful iniquity, from every quarter of the world, pours in and finds a welcome.
>
> First those who acknowledged themselves of this persuasion were arrested; and upon their testimony a vast number were condemned, not so much on the charge of incendiarism, as for their hatred of the human race. Their death was turned into a diversion. They were clothed in the skins of wild beasts, and torn to pieces by dogs; they were fastened to crosses, or set up to be burned, so as to serve the purpose of lamps when daylight failed. Nero gave up his own gardens for this spectacle; he provided also Circensian games, during which he mingled with the populace, or took his stand upon a chariot, in the garb of a charioteer. But guilty as these men were and worthy of direst punishment, the fact that they were being sacrificed for no public good, but only to glut the cruelty of one man, aroused a feeling of pity on their behalf. (Tacitus, *Annals*)

In these words the Christians enter Roman history, tormented, scorned, and misrepresented. An uncompromising conscience had withdrawn the followers of Christ from participation in many of the activities of a society which was much more communal and closely knit than that of the Anglo-Saxon world of today. The crowd had marked the abstinence, reacted as crowds react, and branded the abstainers with its disapproval. Crowds are feeble in reasoning and passionate in imagination. Hence, too often, the sad fate of minorities. Nero, like a hundred demagogues before and after him, seized on the ill-considered emotions of the mass. Nero caught up the dislike which the compliant and conforming majority feel for the dissident and nonconforming few. The spectacle of moral earnestness, such is human nature, offends the morally inert, and the sight of disciplined living rebukes and angers self-indulgence. The vested interests of vice fear virtue, and corruption is uneasy in the presence of a sterner and challenging uprightness. So, in varied fashion, had Christians stirred the emotional hostility of the ancient crowd. Nero channeled the crowd's passion, gave it self-expression, and supplied a cover of logic for baseness, and a cloak of social righteousness for unreasoning hatred.

Social ostracism, therefore, in the early history of the church preceded official persecution. The Christian was at odds with society before he fell out with the State. From the New Testament it is possible to shed some light on the cruel dilemma in which he was placed, and to unearth evidence of an inner conflict which all but shattered the Church. The study of the situation throws light on the principles of persecution and directs attention to some laws of Christian sociology which are by way of finding new importance in the growing paganism of the day. As Professor Butterfield remarks in a significant passage: "We are back for the first time in something like the earliest centuries of Christianity, and those centuries afford some relevant clues to the kind of attitude to adopt."

The reason why we have lingered over this phrase is too obvious for further words.

(b) ". . . denying the power thereof." The power of the Gospel consists in its divine Christ, God's last word to men, crucified, dead and buried to rise again for our justification. Christianity ceases to be Christianity if Christ is diminished or dethroned, the Resurrection denied, and the Bible denuded of its authority. Ephesus had its dissidents. What of today?

6. Some local incident may be in Paul's mind. Irenaeus tells of a charlatan in his day, who specialized in the deception of women. He was suave and elegant and professed to teach his victims to prophesy: "Open your mouth," he would say, "speak whatever occurs to you. You will prophesy." To "prophesy," of course, in Irenaeus' context, means speak under inspiration. But is there not a familiar modern ring in the disreputable story?

7. And in this verse, too. We obviously have here the beginnings of the various Gnostic cults. This is what makes the Epistles of John, written thirty years later to the same Ephesus, such instructive reading. We can catch the situation at Ephesus at various points — in Acts, in Ephesians, in Revelation, in John's first letter.

8. We have already among us, says Paul, modern specimens of the age-old imposter, the court magicians of Pharaoh, who withstood Moses and Aaron. They are not named in Exodus, but a mass of legend grew up around them.

9. But falsehood, says Paul, establishing a principle of history, cannot live forever. As Abraham Lincoln said, all the people cannot be deceived all the time.

B. *Verses 10 to 17*

10. The defeat of falsehood is best effected by the demonstration of the truth. Paul uses a striking word as he turns to appeal to Timothy in the name of the common past. NEB best translates it: "But you have followed me step by step. . . ." Perhaps we could render the verse: "But you have been by my side in what I have taught, in how I have lived, in my vision of what might be. . . ." The word means "to follow alongside."

Paul lists nine features of his Christian testimony. Examine each in turn, for they are facets of our testimony. Every Christian is an example to someone, whether he wishes to be or not. Any defect is damaging. It is well to examine frequently in prayer the nine points. Here is a prayer list:

(i) What am I teaching others about Christ?

(ii) What sort of life am I living before men?
(iii) What is my aim in life?
(iv) How truly do I trust and believe in Christ?
(v) How patient am I in the stress and tension of life?
(vi) What of my love, when I read First Corinthians 13?
(vii) How steadfast am I in faith and conduct?
(viii) What is my attitude when I suffer for Christ?
(ix) How do I bear trouble?

11. The trail went back to the cities of the Asia Minor plateau, where Paul had met Timothy. The young man had seen Paul at grips with evil, and had made his choice in view of that stern spectacle.

12. He knew that such trials were the inevitable consequence of such a choice (see Acts 13:14, 45, 50; 14:1, 2, 5, 6, 19, 22). It was after these things that Timothy entered Paul's service.

Paul took Christ seriously. The Lord had said that those who followed Him would inevitably face some form of persecution, and that blessing would follow endurance. Paul had seen this happen both as agent and victim of persecution. He now taught its reality (Matt. 5:10; Acts 14:22; 1 Thess. 3:4).

What must, in the light of this, be our attitude?

(i) Expect opposition to a true, fearless testimony.
(ii) Expect that opposition to take some active form.
(iii) Do not court persecution, but do not flee from it.
(iv) If you have never known it, ask whether your attitude has been too pliant, or compromising.
(v) Expect blessing from it.

13. And expect appearance sometimes to seem to contradict this. Read Psalm 37. The various translators list a shocking catalog of terms: "imposters"; "pretenders"; "swindlers"; "charlatans"; "mountebanks" — how they swarm. All contain the elements of sound translation. The great truth is that, in seeking to deceive, they become their own victims. We become that which is cherished at the core of the

personality — the whole point in the doctrine of regeneration.

14. Let *us* not be deceived but continue in what we have been taught and have proved by our experience, and that of revered teachers.

15. The Bible is the supreme textbook, to be daily studied, followed and tested.

16. There has been some controversy over the correct translation of this verse, the choice, it must be confessed, being sometimes predetermined by the translator's attitude to the inspiration of Scripture. It seems unnecessary here to go into the whole question. Donald Guthrie, in his *Tyndale Commentary* (pp. 163, 164) discusses the matter with his usual care and scholarship, and those interested in the question will find all they need there. His conclusion is: "While not ruling out the possibility of the alternative interpretation, it is rather more in harmony with grammar and syntax to translate, 'All Scripture is inspired by God and profitable . . .' (RSV)." Scripture is essential. It "equips the man of God for everything good" (17) and gives him:

(i) that which he may teach with confidence;
(ii) the salutary searching of his own heart;
(iii) that which will straighten his ways.

Phillips renders ". . . for teaching the faith, correcting error, for resetting the direction of a man's life."

It must be remembered, however, that "reproof" can be directed to the reader.

QUESTIONS FOR DISCUSSION

(i) Method in Bible study.
(ii) Bible study as an aid to prayer.
(iii) "Falsehoods not only disagree with truths, but usually quarrel among themselves." (Daniel Webster)
(iv) Persecution in the modern world.
(v) Popularity and the Christian.
(vi) Relate the prophecies to the modern scene.
(vii) Is it easier to be a Christian today than it was in the last century?
(viii) Prayer and self-examination.

IV

CHAPTER FOUR (1-22)

Introduction and Summary

The relevance of this chapter is twofold: (i) First its timeless value. The Bible is an ancient book written over a long span of centuries. The New Testament itself, from the birth of Christ till John laid down his pen, covered a century, and that century was the one we call the first. The letters we are reading were written nineteen hundred years ago. And yet the Bible is a modern book dealing with the permanence of life, man's age-old sin and rebellion, his problems and their one solution. Here, as in the last chapter, we have the world today. We quoted the first five verses of the last chapter from Taylor's paraphrase by way of introduction to that section. Here are the first five verses of Chapter 4 from the New English Bible: "Before God, and before Christ Jesus who is to judge men living and dead, I charge you solemnly by His coming appearance and His reign, proclaim the message, press it home on all occasions, convenient or inconvenient, use argument, reproof and appeal, with all the patience that the work of teaching requires. For the time will come when they will not stand wholesome teaching, but will follow their own fancy and gather a crowd of teachers to tickle their ears. They will stop their ears to the truth and turn to mythology. But you yourself must keep calm and sane at all times, face hardship, work to spread the gospel, and do all the duties of your calling."

(ii) Secondly, the biographical importance of the

chapter is supreme. How anyone could imagine that this is fiction or second-century forgery passes belief. The piece reads like biography in the most authentic sense of the word. Let us also pray that at life's ending we may be able to echo Paul's testimony. In the truceless war between good and evil he had never compromised, never surrendered, never retreated. In the long race of life he had never wearied, never turned aside from the goal, never paused. So many, like Demas, begin well (Philem. 24), find the course difficult, grow tired, and drop out of the race. The Marathon of life demands all our staying power. Let us not waste strength and energy in spectacular bursts of speed to win the crowd's applause, but run with patience, abandoning impediments, and with the eye forever on the Judge. Faithfully, consistently, fearlessly, Paul had preached the truth of Christ. He had witnessed before the governors of Rome, before Nero himself, before a king, a high priest, the best brains of Athens, magistrates, and common folk. He never swerved from the duty of preaching the Word. He had been loved, hated, helped, betrayed, had known loneliness and loss, and was soon to face death.

A. *Verses 1 to 5*

1 and 2. A solemn word bids Timothy take heed. It is the word of First Timothy 5:21. Our responsibility must be exercised in view of inevitable judgment, a thought to which Paul often returned (Acts 17:31; Rom. 2:16; 1 Cor. 4:5). And the responsibility is the Gospel committed to our care. The revolt against preaching in some ultra-liberal sections of the Church today, is a complete denial of New Testament authority, and the natural consequence of losing what the New Testament calls the Gospel.

The Gospel must be preached with urgency. "In season, and out of season," says KJV literally translating. "Press it home on all occasions, convenient or inconvenient" (NEB). "Dwell upon it continually, welcome or unwelcome" (Knox).

The phrase is an assonance, not meant to open an excuse for unseasonable intrusion, or tactless haste. It simply means — "keep at the task on set occasions and at all other times." Chrysostom commented: "Do not ask yourself, 'Is this a suitable occasion for preaching?' Ask rather, 'Why should not this be a suitable occasion?' Have no limited season. Let it always be your season, not only in peace and security, and when sitting in the Church."

(Read Kipling's poem on the converted cattleman who "wanted to preach Religion" " 'andsome and out of the wet." It is called *Mulholland's Contract*, p. 127 in the Definitive Edition of Kipling's works.)

Paul may have had in mind the fact that preaching is not always confined to vocal occasions. When is the Christian, who is known to be a Christian, *not* preaching?

Note the following points about preaching:

(i) Rebuke has its place. It must not be harsh, self-righteous, cruel. It must be an exercise of faithfulness and humility.

(ii) The preacher's task is not to make his audience comfortable, but to challenge them.

(iii) Words of reproof must be spoken "with consciousness of our common guilt" (Barclay).

(iv) Preaching must not be negative. Exhortation, or encouragement must follow reproof.

(v) And all this with unwearied patience before hardness, lack of response, opposition.

3. And all this in the face of the fact that there will always be the comfortable preacher who will cash in on man's desire to be deceived for comfort's sake.

4. The truth sometimes hurts, is inconvenient, is costly to follow. "A truth which daunts because it is true, is of far more value than the most stimulating of lies" (M. Maeterlinck).

"I don't like those mighty fine preachers who round off their sentences so beautifully that they are sure to roll off the sinner's conscience" (Rowland Hill).

> "I preached as never sure to preach again,
> And as a dying man to dying men."
>
> (R. Baxter)

5. The opening words link with the first words in the

chapter. The word "evangelist" is used in Acts 21:8 and Ephesians 4:11. The evangelist's was a set office, and Timothy was called to it. It did not, as the letter bears witness, preclude administrative functions.

B. *Verses 6 to 8*

6. The same metaphor is found in Philippians 2:17. The drink offering of the Levitical ritual, or the libation of pagan worship is in Paul's mind. He is ready to be "poured out." Seneca, the philosopher and one-time tutor of Nero, died about this time at the hands of the same criminal ruler. Tacitus tells the vivid story of his suicide in his *Annals* (15.64). He cut his veins but the blood ran slowly. Then, writes the historian, "he entered a hot bath, and sprinkling the servants standing by with a little water, he said, 'a libation to God who gives Freedom'."

With Paul it was his own life out-poured — his ardor, genius, culture, devotion, for the time of his "departure" was at hand. The word he uses is literally "unmooring." It appears as a verb at Philippians 1:23, a second echo of this verse in the Philippian letter. The image of the race in the next verse forms a third echo (Phil. 3:13, 14).

7. "The good fight" may be an athletic contest, in line with the next metaphor: "My race is run." Perfect tenses, which are here used, suggest something finally done whose consequences abide. The fight, the race, are over. Victory abides. The faith is kept and stands unshaken.

8. The metaphor of conflict in some athletic game continues to the presentation of the prize. Paul used the figure frequently. (See *Games* in a Bible Dictionary and in *The Zondervan Topical Bible*).

C. *Verses 9 to 22*

A fascinating passage follows which contains cameo biographies of Christians of the early Church.

(i) *Timothy*. The faithful henchman is bidden come to Rome (6, 13, 21), bringing the cloak hastily left at Troas, before the onset of Rome's winter cold. Paul has no doubt that Timothy will come.

(ii) *Demas.* Demas had once run well (Philem. 24). In this small letter he is called a fellow-laborer. In writing to the Colossian church, in the Lycus Valley where Demas lived, a bare mention of his name is made (Col. 4:14). This may have no significance at all. And now Demas appears a third time, a deserter who was gone, recaptured by the pagan society he left. Paul uses the word he used in Romans 12:2. On that occasion, concluding his long argument on faith, Paul turned to conduct and the character which commended the Gospel. He wrote: "I therefore implore you, brothers, in the name of God's mercies, to dedicate your bodies as a living sacrifice, consecrated to God, well-pleasing to Him, which is the worship proper to your nature. And cease trying to adapt yourself to the society you live in, but continue your transformation by the renewing of your mind, to the end that you may test out for yourself the will of God, that namely, which is good, well-pleasing to him, and perfect" (EMB). This had been his life. Demas had been attracted by it. He had found the tug of "the society he lived in" too strong. Perhaps he had followed Christ on a gust of emotion which had chilled amid the cold realities of life. Perhaps unpopularity, love of a pagan woman, fear of some deprivation, the restraining influence of wife or parents . . . Or was it the weariness of middle age, "the destruction that wasteth at noonday" (Psalm 91:6)?

Barclay, who is always intriguing in his speculation about names, ends his leisurely note on Demas with a suggestion which could form the basis of a novel. Demas is short for Demetrius. Imagine that Demas was Demetrius the silversmith of Acts 19, who led the riot against Paul. Imagine the persecutor being converted, like Paul himself, and becoming the Demas who ran well and then defected. Long years later John wrote in a letter (3:12) of a Demetrius who bore a strong decisive witness fo Christ. Is it the same Demetrius, claimed again by Christ? There is no real evidence at all, but just imagine.

One more speculation. In Philemon 24 Demas is mentioned next to Aristarchus who was a Thessalonian. Was

Demetrius a Thessalonian and had he simply gone home? Or gone home to take up politics? Demetrius is a name which occurs twice among the listed politarchs of the northern Greek city.

(iii) *Crescens.* Nothing is known of this disciple. He had no doubt gone on a mission of organization and confirmation to the eastern province named.

(iv) *Titus* was obeying orders, as we have already seen, following his special task in Crete.

(v) *Luke* we know. He was a great historian. He accompanied Paul on his first trip to Rome and described the adventure on the Alexandrian grain-ship brilliantly. To trace a little of his self-effacing labors, go through the "we-passages" in Acts. Look also at Colossians 4:12, Philemon 24 and Second Corinthians 8:18, where Luke is probably the man described so warmly.

(vi) *Mark* was the young man who had quarreled with Paul, probably over the issue of taking the Gospel to Roman Antioch of Pisidia, instead of ministering to the Jews in Perga (see Acts 13:1-13). Perhaps his uncle Barnabas (Col. 4:10), or perhaps his mother Mary (Acts 12:12), pushed him into missionary work, when he was intended to write a Gospel. He caused a split between Paul and Barnabas (Acts 15:36-40). Failure is not final, and here is Mark back in favor. At the time of writing, Mark must have been somewhere on the route between Ephesus and Rome. Timothy would sail from Troas to Neapolis (Acts 16), proceeding thence to Philippi, and by the Via Egnatia to Dyrrachium, over to Brundisium, and by the Via Appia to Rome.

Mark wrote his gospel at Peter's instigation. Paul may have required his presence for similar literary purposes. (See *The Young Man Mark,* or *In the Image of Peter,* by E. M. Blaiklock: Moody Press.)

(vii) *Tychicus.* See Acts 24:4; Colossians 4:7; Ephesians 6:21; Titus 3:12. He was a trusted messenger of Paul. The past tense in v. 12 is an "epistolary" tense, the writer casting his verb in a tense appropriate to the recipient of the letter. "I am sending Tychicus to Ephesus with this letter."

Perhaps he was also intended to function there in Timothy's absence.

(viii) *Alexander,* says Paul "displayed me much evil." He was probably a renegade Christian who gave evidence at Paul's trial. He may be the man of Acts 19:33, 34. The correct reading runs: "The Lord will reward him. . . ." From v. 15 it appears that Alexander's hatred of Paul was a difference over doctrine. It is a sad comment on human nature that the Latin expression *"odium theologicum"* has appeared in the language. It means "theological hatred" and describes the base animosities which theological controversy has so frequently engendered. It is clear enough from the pastoral epistles that the religious leader is intended to stand firmly for his faith and the purity of his doctrine, but certain rules should be observed:

(a) Make sure the issue is a vital one. There is room for difference in matters of minor interpretation.

(b) Analyze motive. Exhibitionism can sometimes be mistaken for zeal and loyalty toward the truth.

(c) Our personal reputation in such matters must not be foremost. It does not matter that one or another should be proved right.

(d) The words of First Corinthians 13 should ever be before our mind.

Paul's difference with Barnabas is described by Luke with a word probably derived from Paul's own account. It is *paroxusmos* ("the sharp contention" KJV) whence English "paroxysm." When he wrote to the Corinthians Paul said that love *"ou paroxunetai"* using the verb connected with the noun of Acts. "Love is not sharp-tempered." Had Paul his difference with the gentle Barnabas painfully in mind? If so Mark's restoration is even more significant.

(ix) *The unnamed.* None stood with Paul at the preliminary hearing. Such prominence was perilous. A gust of loneliness can sometimes chill a faithful heart. G. K. Chesterton caught the thought in the poem we have already mentioned. England's Christian king was standing at bay exactly eleven centuries ago. The disastrous battle at Reading had

just been fought. A mindless horde of barbarians was break-
ing like some polluted sea all round his harassed land —

> *But Alfred up against them bare,*
> *And gripped the ground and grasped the air,*
>   *Staggered and strove to stand.*
> *He bent them back with spear and spade,*
>   *With desperate dyke and wall,*
> *With foemen leaning on his shield,*
> *And roaring on him when he reeled,*
>   *And no help came at all . . .*

You catch the note of despair in the last line? As the battle
thickens that mood can daunt the heart. It is an illusion,
none the less, as Paul said. The Lord was with him.

(x) *Aquila and Priscilla.* Barclay weaves some intriguing speculation around the names of this much traveled and
faithful pair (Acts 18:2; Rom. 16:3; 1 Cor. 16:19). It may
or may not be true. Observe that Prisca is mentioned before
her husband. She was certainly of higher rank, for her name
is that of an ancient Roman family, and Aquila's name looks
like that of a freedman (See W. M. Ramsay: *Saint Paul the
Traveller and Roman Citizen,* pp. 268, 269).

(xi) *Onesiphorus' household.* Onesiphorus was an Ephesian who ministered bravely to Paul in his capacity (1:16-
18; 4:19). We have suggested above that he had died in
Rome. Some disagree. In the apocryphal work *The Acts of
Paul and Thecla,* Onesiphorus appears as a man of Iconium.
One of the same name was martyred in Mysia early in the
second century. Beyond this identification cannot go.

(xii) *Erastus* may have been the city treasurer of
Corinth mentioned in Romans 16:12, or the companion of
Timothy mentioned in Acts 19:22. Paul is picking up the
thread dropped at v. 12 where he is explaining to Timothy
the absence of some of their mutual friends from Rome during his time of crisis and peril.

(xiii) *Trophimus.* Acts 20:4; 21:29; Second Corinthians
8:19-22. He was a trusted Gentile. He had been left at
Miletus sick. "Forgery," remarked Paley drily, "would not
have spared a miracle." Chrysostom's remark is also to the
point: "The apostles could not do everything."

(xiv) *Eubulus.* Nothing is known of this Christian save that he is thus honored.

(xv) *Pudens and Claudia* figure in another of Barclay's ingenious reconstructions. See also Hasting's *Bible Dictionary.* Also for *Linus,* said to be their son.

QUESTIONS FOR DISCUSSION

    (i) Relate the prophecy in this chapter to the modern scene in the Church. Should the Christian be tolerant of destructive doctrine?

    (ii) Tact in preaching.

    (iii) The dire responsibility of Christian preaching.

    (iv) Demas today.

    (v) Mark today ("Failure is not final").

    (vi) What "torch" have we to carry on?

EPILOGUE

One last word, a personal word from the one who has been with you in these study notes. In the introduction to the second letter to Timothy, I used the phrase: "Paul seeks to hand on the torch." It stirred a memory.

Eleven years ago I visited the great American war cemetery at Madingly near England's Cambridge. It was a quiet summer's evening, and it was an awesome sight to see, in the long shadows of the westering sun, amid the beauty of smooth lawns and marble walls, the serried crosses of the multitudinous dead, the silent host who died for our liberty. An inscription around the base of a great bronze hemisphere which held the flagstaff read: TO YOU FROM FAILING HANDS WE THROW THE TORCH. BE YOURS TO HOLD IT HIGH.

The dead in Christ of all the embattled centuries cry to you, young men and women of our church. You will not, I know, fail your generation. Those of us who, through this half century, 'mid noise of war and the world's tumult, have sought to carry the torch, fling it blazing on to you — BE YOURS TO HOLD IT HIGH.